J Krishnamurti

THE BEAUTY OF LIFE

Krishnamurti's Journal

The Beauty of Life
Krishnamurti's Journal

Full-text edition

This edition published in the UK and USA by
Watkins, an imprint of Watkins Media Limited
Unit 11, Shepperton House
89-93 Shepperton Road
London
N1 3DF

enquiries@watkinspublishing.com

kfoundation.org

First edition 1982
Reprinted 1994, 1998
Second, revised edition 2003
Third, revised full-text edition 2023

Editors: Mary Lutyens, Ray McCoy, Duncan Toms

Krishnamurti, J. (1895–1986)

ISBN: 978-1-78678-747-7 (Hardback)
978-1-78678-753-8 (E-book)

Printed and bound in the UK by TJ Books Limited

www.watkinspublishing.com

CONTENTS

INTRODUCTION

ADDITIONAL PAGES TO KRISHNAMURTI'S JOURNAL

In December 2007, 36 pages in Krishnamurti's handwriting were handed to the archivist in Ojai, California by Mary Zimbalist. When Krishnamurti first gave the pages to her, he said they were for the *Journal*.

The dates on these additional pages were not in Krishnamurti's handwriting but had been noted there, probably by Mary, on the dates he gave them to her in 1981. They consisted of 13 new entries, which were first published in Krishnamurti Foundation Trust Bulletins numbered 56 to 61. Mary Lutyens, editor of the first edition of the *Journal*, had received them from Mary Zimbalist and published them in the Bulletins because the first edition of the *Journal* was already in print.

This new full-text edition includes these additional entries, forming a complete *Journal* for the first time.

Ray McCoy

FOREWORD

In September 1973, Krishnamurti suddenly started keeping a journal. For nearly six weeks he made daily entries in a notebook. For the first month of that period, Krishnamurti was staying at Brockwood Park in Hampshire, and for the rest of the time in Rome. He resumed the journal 18 months later while in California.

Nearly every entry starts with a description of a natural scene which he knew intimately, yet in only three instances do these descriptions refer to the place in which he was actually staying. Thus, the first page of the first entry describes the Grove at Brockwood Park, but by the second page, he is evidently in Switzerland in imagination. It is not until he is staying in California in 1975 that he again describes his actual surroundings. For the rest, he is recalling places he has stayed, with a clarity that shows how vivid was his memory for natural scenery, arising from the acuteness of his observation. This journal also reveals to what an extent his teaching was inspired by his closeness to nature.

Throughout, Krishnamurti refers to himself in the third person as 'he', and incidentally he tells us something about himself which he had not done before.

Mary Lutyens

BROCKWOOD PARK

September 14, 1973

That evening, while walking through the wood, we passed through the grove near the big white house. Coming over the stile into the grove, one immediately felt a great sense of peace and stillness. Not a thing was moving. It seemed sacrilegious to walk through it, to tread the ground; it was profane to talk, even to breathe. The great redwood trees were absolutely still. The Native Americans call them the silent ones, and now they were really silent. Even the dog didn't chase the rabbits. You stood still hardly daring to breathe; you felt you were an intruder, for you had been chatting and laughing, and to enter this grove not knowing what lay there was a surprise and a shock, the shock of an unexpected benediction. The heart was beating less fast, speechless with the wonder of it. It was the centre of this whole place. Every time you enter it now, there is that beauty, that stillness, that strange stillness. Come when you will and it will be there, full, rich and unnameable.

Any form of conscious meditation is not the real thing; it can never be. Deliberate attempt to meditate is not meditation. It must happen; it cannot be invited. Meditation is not the play of the mind nor of desire and pleasure. All attempt to meditate is the very denial of it. Only be aware of what you are thinking and doing and of nothing else. The seeing, the hearing, is the doing, without reward and punishment—the skill in doing lies in the skill of seeing, hearing. Every form of meditation leads inevitably to deception, to illusion, for desire blinds.

It was a lovely evening, and the soft light of spring covered the earth.

September 15, 1973

It is good to be alone. To be far away from the world and yet walk its streets is to be alone. To be alone walking up the path beside the rushing, noisy mountain stream full of spring water and melting snows is to be aware of that solitary tree, alone in its beauty. The loneliness of a man in the street is the pain of life; he is never alone, far away, untouched and vulnerable. To be full of knowledge is never to be alone, and the activity of that knowledge breeds endless misery. The demand for expression, with its frustrations and pains, is that man who walks the streets; he is never alone. Sorrow is the movement of that loneliness.

That mountain stream was full and high with the melting snows and the rains of early spring. You could hear big boulders being pushed around by the force of onrushing waters. A tall pine of fifty years or more crashed into the water; the road was being washed away. The stream was muddy, slate coloured. The fields above it were full of wildflowers. The air was pure, and there was enchantment. On the high hills, there was still snow, and the glaciers and the great peaks still held the recent snows; they will still be white all the summer long.

It was a marvellous morning, and you could have walked on endlessly, never feeling the steep hills. There was a perfume in the air, clear and strong. There was no one on that path, coming down or going up; you were alone with those dark pines and the rushing waters. The sky was that astonishing blue that only the mountains have. You looked at it through leaves and the straight pines. There was no one to talk to, and there was no chattering of the mind. A magpie, white and black, flew by, disappearing into the woods. The path led away from the noisy stream, and the silence was absolute. It wasn't the silence after the noise; it wasn't the silence that comes with the setting of the sun, nor that silence when the mind dies down. It wasn't the silence of museums and churches but something totally unrelated to time and space. It wasn't the silence that mind makes for itself. The sun was hot, and the shadows were pleasant.

He discovered only recently that there was not a single thought during these long walks, in the crowded streets or on the solitary paths. Ever since he was a boy, it had been like that: no thought entered his mind. He was watching and listening and nothing else. Thought with its associations never arose; there was no image-making. One day he was suddenly aware of how extraordinary it was; he often attempted to think, but no thought would come. On these walks, with people or without them, any movement of thought was absent. This is to be alone.

Over the snow peaks, clouds were forming, heavy and dark; probably it would rain later on, but now the shadows were very sharp with the sun bright and clear. There was still that pleasant smell in the air, and the rains would bring a different smell. It was a long way down to the chalet.

September 16, 1973

At that time of the morning, the streets of the small village were empty, but beyond them the country was full with trees, meadows and whispering breezes. The main street was lit, and everything else was in darkness. The sun would come up in about three hours. It was a clear starlit morning. The snow peaks and the glaciers were still in darkness, and almost everyone was sleeping. The narrow mountain roads had so many curves that one couldn't go very fast; the car was new and being run-in. It was a beautiful car, powerful with good lines. In that morning air, the motor ran most efficiently. On the autoroute it was a thing of beauty and as it climbed it took every corner, steady as a rock. The dawn was there, the shape of the trees and the long line of hills and the vineyards; it was going to be a lovely morning; it was cool and pleasant among the hills. The sun was up and there was dew on the leaves and meadows.

He always liked machinery; he dismantled the motor of a car, and when it ran it was as good as new. When you are driving, meditation seems to come so naturally. You are aware of the countryside, the houses, the farmers in the field, the make of the passing car and the blue sky through the leaves. You are not even aware that meditation is going on; this meditation that began ages ago and would go on endlessly. Time is not a factor in meditation, nor the word which is the meditator. There is no meditator in meditation. If there is, it is not meditation. The meditator is the word, thought and time, and so subject to change, to the coming and going. It is not a flower that blooms and dies. Time is movement. You are sitting on the bank of a river, watching the waters, the current and the things floating by. When you are in the water, there is no watcher. Beauty is not in the mere expression; it is in the abandonment of the word and expression, the canvas and the book.

How peaceful the hills, the meadows and these trees are: the whole country is bathed in the light of a passing morning. Two men are arguing loudly with many gestures, red in the face. The road runs through a long avenue of trees and the tenderness of the morning is fading. The sea stretches before you, and the smell of eucalyptus is in the air.

He was a short man, lean and hard of muscle; he had come from a faraway country, darkened by the sun. After a few words of greeting, he launched into criticism. How easy it is to criticise without knowing what actually are the facts. He said, 'You may be free and really live all that you are talking about, and I am sure of this. But physically you are in a prison, padded by your friends. You don't know what is happening around you. People have assumed authority, though you yourself are not authoritarian.'

I am not sure you are right in this matter. To run a school or anything, there must be a certain responsibility, and it can and does exist without the authoritarian implication. Authority is wholly detrimental to cooperation, to talking things over together. This is what is being done in all the work that we are engaged in. This is an actual fact. If one may point out, no one comes between me and another.

'What you are saying is of the utmost importance. All that you write and say should be printed and circulated by a small group of people who are serious and dedicated. The world is exploding, and it is passing you by.'

I am again afraid you are not fully aware of what is happening. At one time a small group took the responsibility of circulating what was being said, and they themselves printed the talks. Now, too, a small group has undertaken the same responsibility. Again, if one may point out, you are not aware of what is going on.

He made various other criticisms, but they were based on assumptions and passing opinions. Without defending, one pointed out what was actually taking place. But—

How strange human beings are.

The hills were receding, and the noise of daily life was around one, the coming and the going, sorrow and pleasure. A single tree on a hillock was the beauty of the land. And deep down in the valley was a stream and beside it ran a railroad. You must leave the world to see the beauty of that stream.

September 17, 1973

That evening, walking through the wood, there was a feeling of menace. The sun was just setting and the palm trees were solitary against the golden western sky. The monkeys were in the banyan tree, getting ready for the night. Hardly anyone used that path, and rarely you met another human being. There were many deer, shy and disappearing into the thick growth. Yet the menace was there, heavy and pervading; it was all around you, you looked over your shoulder. There were no dangerous animals; they had moved away; it was too close to the sprawling town. One was glad to leave and walk back through the lighted streets. But the next evening the monkeys were still there and so were the deer and the sun was just behind the tallest trees; the menace was gone. On the contrary, the trees, the bushes and the small plants welcomed you. You were among your friends; you felt completely safe and most welcome. The woods accepted you, and every evening it was a pleasure to walk there.

Forests are different. There is physical danger there, not only from snakes but from tigers that were known to be there. As one walked there one afternoon, suddenly there was an abnormal silence; the birds stopped chattering, the monkeys were absolutely still, and everything seemed to be holding its breath. One stood still. And as suddenly, everything came to life; the monkeys were playing and teasing each other, birds began their evening chatter, and one was aware the danger had passed.

In the woods where man kills rabbits, pheasants and squirrels, there is quite a different atmosphere. You are entering into a world where man has been, with his gun and peculiar violence. Then the woods lose their tenderness, their welcome, and some beauty has been lost, and that happy whisper has gone.

You have only one head and look after it for it is a marvellous thing. No machinery, no computer can compare with it. It is so vast, so complex, so utterly capable, subtle and productive. It is the storehouse of experience, knowledge and memory; all thought springs from it. What it has put together is quite incredible: mischief, confusion, sorrow, wars, corruption, illusions, ideals, pain and misery, the great cathedrals, the lovely mosques and the sacred temples. It is fantastic what it has done and what it can do. But one thing it apparently cannot do is completely change its behaviour in its relationship to another head, another man. Neither punishment nor reward seems to change its behaviour; knowledge does not seem to transform its conduct. The *me* and the *you* remain. It never realises that the *me* is the *you*, that the observer is the observed. Its love is its degeneration; its pleasure is its agony; the gods of its ideals are its destroyers. Its freedom is its own prison and it is educated to live in this prison, only making it more comfortable, more pleasurable. You have only one head, care for it, don't destroy it. It is so easy to poison it.

He always had this strange lack of distance between himself and the trees, rivers and mountains. It wasn't cultivated; you cannot cultivate a thing like that. There was never a wall between him and another. What they did to him, what they said to him never seemed to wound him, nor flattery to touch him. Somehow he was untouched. He was not withdrawn or aloof but like the waters of a river. He had so few thoughts; no thoughts at all when he was alone. His brain was active when talking or writing, but otherwise it was quiet and active without movement. Movement is time, and activity is not.

This strange activity, without direction, seems to go on, sleeping or waking. He wakes up often with that activity of meditation; something of this nature is going on most of the time. He never rejected it or invited it. The other night he woke up, wide awake. He was aware that something like a ball of fire, light, was being put into his head, into the very centre of it. He watched it objectively for a considerable time, as though it were happening to someone else. It was not an illusion, something conjured up by the mind.

Dawn was coming, and through the opening of the curtains he could see the trees.

September 18, 1973

It is still one of the most beautiful valleys. It is entirely
surrounded by hills and filled with orange groves. Many
years ago there were very few houses among the trees and
orchards, but now there are many more; the roads are
wider, there is more traffic and more noise, especially at
the west end of the valley. But the hills and high peaks
remain the same, untouched by man. There are many
trails leading to the high mountains, and one walked
endlessly along them. One met bears, rattlesnakes, deer
and once a bobcat. The bobcat was ahead, down the
narrow trail, purring and rubbing himself against rocks
and the short trunks of trees. The breeze was coming up
the canyon and so one could get quite close to him. He
was really enjoying himself, delighted with his world. His
short tail was up, his pointed ears straight forward, his
russet hair bright and clean, and he was totally unaware
that someone was just behind him about twenty feet away.
We went down the trail for about a mile, neither of us
making the least sound. It was really a beautiful animal,
sprightly and graceful. There was a narrow stream ahead
of us and wishing not to frighten him when we came to it,
one whispered a gentle greeting. He never looked round,
that would have been a waste of time, but streaked off,
completely disappearing in a few seconds. We had been
friends, though, for a considerable time.

The valley is filled with the smell of orange blossom, almost overpowering, especially in the early mornings and evenings. It was in the room, in the valley and in every corner of the earth, and the god of flowers blessed the valley. It would be really hot in the summer, and that had its own peculiarity. Many years ago, when one went there, there was a marvellous atmosphere; it is still there to a lesser degree. Human beings are spoiling it as they seem to spoil most things. It will be as before. A flower may wither and die, but it will come back with its loveliness.

Have you ever wondered why human beings go wrong, become corrupt, indecent in their behaviour—aggressive, violent and cunning? It is no good blaming the environment, the culture or the parents. We want to put the responsibility for this degeneration on others or on some happening. Explanations and causes are an easy way out. The ancient Hindus called it karma, what you sowed you reaped. The psychologists put the problem in the lap of the parents. What the so-called religious people say is based on their dogma and belief. But the question is still there.

Then there are others, born generous, kind, responsible. They are not changed by the environment or any pressure. They remain the same in spite of all the clamour. Why?

Any explanation is of little significance. All explanations are escapes, avoiding the reality of *what is*. This is the only thing that matters. The *what is* can be totally transformed with the energy that is wasted in explanations and in searching out the causes. Love is not in time nor in analysis, in regrets and recriminations. It is there when desire for money, position and the cunning deceit of the self are not.

September 19, 1973

The monsoon had set in. The sea was almost black under the dark heavy clouds, and the wind was tearing at the trees. It would rain for a few days, torrential rains, and it would stop for a day or so, to begin again. Frogs were croaking in every pond and the pleasant smell the rains brought filled the air. The earth was clean again, and in a few days it became astonishingly green. Things grew almost under your eyes; the sun would come, and all the things of the earth would be sparkling. Early in the morning, there would be chanting. The small squirrels were all over the place. There were flowers everywhere, the wild ones and the cultivated, the jasmine, the rose and the marigold.

One day on the road that leads to the sea, while one walked under the palms and the heavy rain trees, looking at a thousand things, a group of children were singing. They seemed so happy, innocent and utterly unaware of the world. One of them recognised us, came smiling and we walked hand in hand for some time. Neither of us said a word, and as we came near her house she saluted and disappeared inside. The world and the family are going to destroy her, and she will have children too, cry over them, and in the cunning ways of the world, they will be destroyed. But that evening, she was happy and eager to share it by holding a hand.

When the rains had gone, returning on the same road one evening when the western sky was golden, one passed a young man carrying a fire in an earthenware pot. He was bare except for his clean loincloth, and behind him two men were carrying a dead body. All were Brahmins, freshly washed, clean, holding themselves upright, walking quite fast. The young man carrying the fire must have been the son of the dead man. The body was going to be cremated on some secluded sands. It was all so simple, unlike the elaborate hearse, loaded with flowers, followed by a long line of polished cars or mourners walking behind the coffin: the dark blackness of it all. Or you saw a dead body, decently covered, being carried at the back of a bicycle to the sacred river to be burnt.

Death is everywhere, and we never seem to live with it. It is a dark, frightening thing to be avoided, never to be talked of. Keep it away from the closed door. But it is always there. The beauty of love is death, and one knows neither. Death is pain and love is pleasure, and the two can never meet; they must be kept apart, and the division is the pain and agony. This has been from the beginning of time, the division and the endless conflict. There will always be death for those who do not see that the observer is the observed, the experiencer is the experienced. It is like a vast river in which man is caught, with all his worldly goods, his vanities, pains and knowledge. Unless he leaves all the things he has accumulated in the river and swims ashore, death will always be at his door, waiting and watching. When he leaves the river, there is no shore; the bank is the word, the observer. He has left everything, the river and the bank. For the river is time and the banks are the thoughts of time; the river is the movement of time, and thought is of it. When the observer leaves everything of which he is, then the observer is not. This is not death. It is the timeless. You cannot know it, for what is known is of time; you cannot experience it: recognition is made up of time. Freedom from the known is freedom from time. Immortality is not the word, the book, the image you have put together. The soul, the *me*, the atman is the child of thought which is time. When time is not, then death is not. Love is.

The western sky had lost its colour and just over the horizon was the new moon, young, shy and tender. On the road, everything seemed to be passing: marriage, death, the laughter of children and someone sobbing. Near the new moon was a single star.

September 20, 1973

The river was particularly beautiful this morning; the sun was just coming over the trees and the village hidden among them. The air was very still and there was not a ripple on the water. It would get quite warm during the day but now it was rather cool, and a solitary monkey was sitting in the sun. It was always there by itself, big and heavy. During the day it disappeared and turned up early in the morning on the top of the tamarind tree; when it got warm, the tree seemed to swallow it. The golden green flycatchers were sitting on the parapet with the doves, and the vultures were on the top branches of another tamarind. There was immense quietness, and one sat on a bench, lost to the world.

Coming back from the airport on a shaded road with the parrots, green and red, screeching around the trees, one saw across the road what appeared to be a large bundle. As the car came near, the bundle turned out to be a man lying right across the road, almost naked. The car stopped and we got out. His body was large and his head very small; he was staring through the leaves at the astonishingly blue sky. We looked up too to see what he was staring at and the sky from the road was really blue and the leaves were really green. He was malformed, and they said he was one of the village idiots. He never moved and the car had to be driven around him very carefully. The camels with their load and the shouting children passed him without paying the least attention. A dog passed, making a wide circle. The parrots were busy with their noise. The dry fields, the villagers, the trees, the yellow flowers were occupied with their own existence. That part of the world was underdeveloped, and there was no one or organisation to look after such people. There were open gutters, filth and crowding humanity, and the sacred river went on its way. The sadness of life was everywhere and in the blue sky, high in the air, were the heavy-winged vultures, circling without moving their wings, circling by the hour, waiting and watching.

What are sanity and insanity? Who is sane and who is insane? Are the politicians sane? The priests, are they insane? Those who are committed to ideologies, are they sane? We are controlled, shaped, pushed around by them, and are we sane?

What is sanity? To be whole, non-fragmented in action, in life, in every kind of relationship—that is the very essence of sanity. Sanity means to be whole, healthy and holy. To be insane, neurotic, psychotic, unbalanced, schizophrenic, whatever name you might give to it, is to be fragmented, broken-up in action and in the movement of relationship which is existence. To breed antagonism and division, which is the trade of the politicians who represent you, is to cultivate and sustain insanity, whether they are dictators or those in power in the name of peace or some form of ideology. And the priest! Look at the world of priesthood. He stands between you and what he and

you consider truth, Saviour, God, heaven, hell. He is the
interpreter, the representative; he holds the keys to heaven;
he has conditioned man through belief, dogma and ritual;
he is the real propagandist. He has conditioned you because
you want comfort and security, and you dread tomorrow.
The artists and the intellectuals—are they sane? Or do
they live in two different worlds—the world of ideas and
imagination with its compulsive expression, wholly separate
from their daily life of sorrow and pleasure?

The world about you is fragmented and so are you, and
its expression is conflict, confusion and misery. You are the
world and the world is you. Sanity is to live a life of action
without conflict. Action and idea are contradictory. Seeing
is the doing and not ideation first and action according
to the conclusion, which breeds conflict. The analyser
himself is the analysed. When the analyser separates himself
as something different from the analysed, he then begets
conflict, and conflict is the area of the unbalanced. The
observer is the observed and therein lies sanity, the whole,
and with the holy is love.

September 21, 1973

It is good to wake up without a single thought, with its problems. Then the mind is rested; it has brought about order within itself, and that is why sleep is so important. Either the mind brings about order in its relationship and action during the waking hours, which gives to it complete rest during sleep, or during sleep it attempts to arrange its affairs to its own satisfaction. During the day there will again be disorder caused by so many factors, and during the hours of sleep the mind will try to extricate itself from this confusion. Mind, brain, can only function efficiently, objectively, where there is order. Conflict in any form is disorder. Consider what the mind goes through every day of its life: the attempt at order in sleep, and disorder during waking hours. This is the conflict of life, day in, day out. The brain can only function in security, not in contradiction and confusion. So it tries to find it in some neurotic formula, but the conflict becomes worse. Order is the transformation of all this mess. When the observer is the observed there is complete order.

In the little lane that goes by the house, shaded and quiet, a little girl was sobbing her heart out, as only children can do. She must have been 5 or 6, small for her age. She was sitting on the ground, tears pouring down her cheeks, and she could hardly breathe with her sobbing. He sat down with her and asked what had happened, but she couldn't talk; sobbing took all her breath. She must have

been struck, or her favourite toy broken, or something
which she wanted denied by a harsh word. The mother
came out, shook the child and carried her in. She barely
looked at him for they were strangers. A few days later,
walking along the same lane, the child came out of her
house, full of smiles, and walked with him a little way.
The mother must have given her permission to go with a
stranger. He often walked in that shady lane, and the girl
with her brother and sister would come out and greet him.
Will they ever forget their hurts and their sorrows, or will
they gradually build for themselves escapes and resistances?
To keep these hurts seems to be the nature of human
beings, and from this their actions become twisted.

Can the human mind never be hurt, wounded? Not
to be hurt is to be innocent. If you are not hurt, you will
naturally not hurt another. Is this possible? The culture
in which we live does deeply wound the mind and heart.
The noise and pollution, the aggression and competition,
the violence and education—all these and more
contribute to the agony. Yet we have to live in this world
of brutality and resistance: we are the world and the world
is us. What is the thing that is hurt? The image that each
one has built about himself, that is what is hurt. Strangely
these images all over the world are the same, with some
modifications. The essence of the image you have is the
same as of the man a thousand miles away. So you are that
man or woman. Your hurts are the hurts of thousands;
you are the other.

Is it possible never to be hurt? Where there is a wound, there is no love. Where there is hurt, love is mere pleasure. When you discover for yourself the beauty of never being hurt, then only do all the past hurts disappear. In the full present, the past has lost its burden.

He has never been hurt though many things happened to him, flattery and insult, threat and security. It is not that he was insensitive, unaware; he had no image of himself, no conclusion, no ideology. Image is resistance, and when that is not, there is vulnerability but no hurt. You may not seek to be vulnerable, highly sensitive, for that which is sought and found is another form of the same image. Understand this whole movement, not merely verbally, but have an insight into it. Be aware of the whole structure of it without any reservation. Seeing the truth of it is the ending of the image-builder.

The pond was overflowing, and there were a thousand reflections on it. It became dark, and the heavens were open.

September 22, 1973

A woman was singing next door; she had a marvellous voice, and the few who were listening to her were entranced. The sun was setting among the mango trees and palms, rich golden and green. She was singing devotional songs, and the voice was getting richer and mellower. Listening is an art. When you listen to classical western music or to this woman, sitting on the floor, you are being romantic, or there are remembrances of things past, or thought with its associations is swiftly changing your moods, or there are intimations of the future. Or you listen without any movement of thought. You listen out of complete quietness, out of total silence.

Listening to one's thought or to the blackbird on a branch, or to what is being said, without the response of thought, brings about a wholly different significance from that which the movement of thought brings. This is the art of listening, listening with total attention: there is no centre which listens.

The silence of the mountains has a depth which the valleys have not. Each has its own silence; the silence among clouds and among trees is vastly different; the silence between two thoughts is timeless; the silence of pleasure and fear are tangible. The artificial silence which thought can manufacture is death; the silence between noises is the absence of noise, but it is not silence, as the absence of war is not peace. The dark silence of a cathedral or temple is of age and beauty, especially constructed by man; there is the silence of the past and future, the silence of the museum and the cemetery. But all this is not silence.

The man was sitting on the bank of the beautiful river, motionless; he was there for over an hour. He would come there every morning, freshly bathed. He would chant in Sanskrit for some time, and presently he would be lost in his thoughts; he didn't seem to mind the sun, at least the morning sun. One day he came to visit and began to talk about meditation. He did not belong to any school of meditation; he considered them useless, without any great significance. He was alone, unmarried and had put away the ways of the world long ago. He had controlled his desires, shaped his thoughts and lived a solitary life. He was not bitter, vain or indifferent; he had forgotten all these some years ago. Meditation and reality were his life.

As he talked and groped for the right word, the sun was setting, and deep silence descended upon us. He stopped talking. After a while, when the stars were very close to the earth, he said, 'That is the silence I have been looking for everywhere, in books, among teachers and in myself. I have found many things but not this. It came unsought, uninvited. Have I wasted my life in things that did not matter? You have no idea what I have been through, the fasting, the selfdenials and the practices. I saw their futility

long ago but never came upon this silence. What shall
I do to remain in it, to maintain it, to hold it in my heart?
I suppose you would say do nothing, as one cannot invite
it. But shall I go on wandering over this country, with
this repetition, this control? Sitting here, I am conscious
of this sacred silence. Through it, I look at the stars, those
trees, the river. Though I see and feel all this, I am not
really there. As you said the other day, the observer is
the observed. I see what it means now. The benediction
I sought is not to be found in the seeking. It is time for me
to go.'

The river became dark and the stars were reflected on its
waters near the banks. Gradually the noises of the day were
coming to an end and the soft noises of the night began.
You watched the stars, and the dark earth and the world
were far away. Beauty, which is love, seemed to descend on
the earth and the things of it.

September 23, 1973

He was standing by himself on the low bank of the river; it was not very wide, and he could see some people on the other bank. If their talk was loud, he could almost hear them. In the rainy season, the river met the open waters of the sea. It had been raining for days and the river had broken through the sands to the waiting sea. With the heavy rains, it was clean again and one could swim in it safely. The river was wide enough to hold a long narrow island, green with bushes, a few short trees and a small palm. When the water was not too deep, cattle would wade across to graze on it. It was a pleasant and friendly river, and it was particularly so on that morning.

He was standing there with no one around, alone, unattached and far away. He was about 14 or less. They had found his brother and himself quite recently, and all the fuss and sudden importance given to him was around him. He was the centre of respect and devotion, and in the years to come he would be the head of organisations and great properties. All that and the dissolution of them still lay ahead. Standing there alone, lost and strangely aloof, was his first and lasting remembrance of those days and events. He doesn't remember his childhood, the schools and the caning. He was told years later by the very teacher who hurt him that he used to cane him practically every day. He would cry and be put out on the veranda until the school closed, and the teacher would come out and ask him to go home; otherwise he would still be on the veranda, lost. He was caned, this man said, because he couldn't study or remember anything he had read or been told. Later the teacher couldn't believe that boy was the man who had given the talk he had heard. He was greatly surprised and unnecessarily respectful.

All those years passed without leaving scars or memories on his mind; his friendships, his affections, even those years with those two who had ill-treated him. Somehow none of these events, friendly or brutal, have left marks on him. In recent years, a writer asked if he could recall all those rather strange events, how he and his brother were discovered and so on, and when he replied that he could not remember them and could only repeat what others had said, the man openly, with a sneer, stated that he was putting it on and pretending. He never consciously blocked any happening, pleasant or unpleasant, entering into his mind. They came, leaving no mark and passed away.

Consciousness is its content: the content makes up consciousness. The two are indivisible. There is no you and another, only the content which makes up consciousness as the *me* and the *not me*. The contents vary according to culture, the racial accumulations, the techniques and capacities acquired. These are broken-up as the artist, the scientist and so on. Idiosyncrasies are the response of the conditioning, and the conditioning is the common factor of man. This conditioning is the content, consciousness. This again is broken up as the conscious and the hidden. The hidden becomes important because we have never looked at it as a whole. This fragmentation takes place when the observer is not the observed, when the experiencer is seen as different from the experience. The hidden is as the open; the observation—the hearing of the open—is the seeing of the hidden. Seeing is not analysing. In analysing there is the analyser and the analysed, a fragmentation which leads to inaction, a paralysis. In seeing, the observer is not, and so action is immediate; there is no interval between the idea and action. The idea, the conclusion, is the observer—the seer separate from the thing seen. Identification is an act of thought, and thought is fragmentation.

The island, the river and the sea, the palms and the buildings, are still there. The sun was coming out of masses of clouds, serried and soaring to the heavens. In only loincloths, the fishermen were throwing their nets to catch some measly little fish. Unwilling poverty is a degradation. Late in the evening, it was pleasant among the mangoes and scented flowers. How beautiful is the earth.

September 24, 1973

A new consciousness and a totally new morality are necessary to bring about a radical change in the present culture and social structure. This is obvious, yet the left and the right and the revolutionary seem to disregard it. Any dogma, any formula, any ideology, is part of the old consciousness; they are the fabrications of thought whose activity is fragmentation—the left, the right, the centre. This activity will inevitably lead to bloodshed of the right or of the left, or to totalitarianism. This is what is going on around us. One sees the necessity of social, economic and moral change, but the response is from the old consciousness, thought being the principal actor. The mess, the confusion and the misery that human beings have got into are within the area of the old consciousness, and without changing that profoundly, every human activity, political, economic and religious, will only bring us to the destruction of each other and of the earth. This is so obvious to the sane.

One has to be a light to oneself; this light is the law. There is no other law. All other laws are made by thought and so fragmentary and contradictory. To be a light to oneself is not to follow the light of another, however reasonable, logical, historical, and however convincing. You cannot be a light to yourself if you are in the dark shadows of authority, of dogma, of conclusion. Morality is not put together by thought; it is not the outcome of environmental pressure; it is not of yesterday, of tradition. Morality is the child of love, and love is not desire and pleasure. Sexual or sensory enjoyment is not love.

High in the mountains, there were hardly any birds; there were some crows, there were deer and an occasional bear. The huge redwoods, the silent ones, were everywhere, dwarfing all other trees. It was a magnificent country and utterly peaceful, for no hunting was allowed. Every animal, every tree and flower was protected. Sitting under one of those massive redwoods, one was aware of the history of man and the beauty of the earth. A fat red squirrel passed by most elegantly, stopping a few feet away, watching and wondering what you were doing there. The earth was dry, though there was a stream nearby. Not a leaf stirred, and the beauty of silence was among the trees. Going slowly along the narrow path, round the bend was a bear with four cubs as large as big cats. They rushed off to crawl up trees, and the mother faced one without a movement, without a sound. About fifty feet separated us; she was enormous, brown, and prepared. One immediately turned one's back on her and left. Each understood that there was no fear and no intention to hurt, but all the same, one was glad to be among the protecting trees, squirrels and the scolding jays.

Freedom is to be a light to oneself; then it is not an abstraction, a thing conjured by thought. Actual freedom is freedom from dependency, attachment, from the craving for experience. Freedom from the very structure of thought is to be a light to oneself. In this light all action takes place, and thus it is never contradictory. Contradiction only exists when that law, light, is separate from action, when the actor is separate from action. The ideal, the principle, is the barren movement of thought and cannot coexist with this light; one denies the other. This light, this law, is separate from you; where the observer is, this light, this love, is not. The structure of the observer is put together by thought, which is never new, never free. There is no *how*, no system, no practice. There is only the seeing which is the doing. You have to see, not through the eyes of another. This light, this law, is neither yours nor that of another. There is only light. This is love.

September 25, 1973

He was looking out of the window on to the green rolling
hills and dark woods with the morning sun on them. It
was a pleasant and lovely morning; there were magnificent
clouds beyond the woods, white with billowing shapes. No
wonder the ancients said the gods had their abode among
them and the mountains. All around there were these
enormous clouds against a blue and dazzling sky. He had
not a single thought and was only looking at the beauty
of the world. He must have been at that window for some
time, and something took place, unexpected and uninvited.
You cannot invite or desire such things, unknowingly or
consciously. Everything seemed to withdraw and be giving
space only to that, the unnameable. You won't find it in
any temple, mosque or church or on any printed page. You
will find it nowhere, and whatever you find, it is not that.

With so many others in that vast structure near the Golden
Horn, he was sitting next to a beggar with torn rags, head
lowered, uttering some prayer. A man began to sing in Arabic.
He had a marvellous voice. The entire dome and great edifice
was filled with it; it seemed to shake the building. It had a
strange effect on all those who were there; they listened to
the words and the voice with great respect and were at the
same time enchanted. He was a stranger amongst them;
they looked at him and then forgot him. The vast hall was
filled, and presently there was a silence; they went through
their ritual and one by one they left. Only the beggar and he

40

remained; then the beggar too left. The great dome was silent and the edifice became empty, the noise of life far away.

If you ever walk by yourself high in the mountains among the pines and rocks, leaving everything in the valley far below you, when there is not a whisper among the trees and every thought has withered away, then it may come to you, the otherness. If you hold it, it will never come again; what you hold is the memory of it dead and gone. What you hold is not the real; your heart and mind are too small, they can hold only the things of thought and that is barren. Go further away from the valley, far away, leaving everything down there. You can come back and pick them up if you want to, but they will have lost their weight. You will never be the same again.

After a long climb of several hours, beyond the treeline, he was there among rocks and the silence only mountains have. There were a few stunted and misshaped pines. There was no wind, and everything was utterly still. Walking back, moving from rock to rock, he suddenly heard a rattler and jumped. A few feet away was the snake, fat and almost black. With the rattle in the middle of the coils, it was ready to strike. The triangular head with its forked tongue flickering in and out, its dark, sharp eyes watching, it was ready to strike if he moved nearer. It had given a warning; it had done its duty, and it was up to you if you came nearer. During all that half hour or more, it never blinked, it stared at you; it had no eyelids. Uncoiling slowly, keeping

41

its head and tail towards him, it began to move away in a U-shape and when he made a move to get nearer it coiled up instantly ready to strike. We played this game for a little while; it was getting tired and he left it to go its own way. It was a really frightening thing, fat and deadly.

You must be alone with the trees, meadows and streams. You are never alone if you carry the things of thought, its images and problems. The mind must not be filled with the rocks and clouds of the earth. It must be empty as the newly-made vessel. Then you would see something totally, something that has never been. You cannot see this if you are there; you must die to see it. You may think you are the important thing in the world, but you are not. You may have everything that thought has put together, but they are all old, used, and begin to crumble.

In the valley, it was surprisingly cool. Near the huts, the squirrels were waiting for their nuts. They had been fed every day in the cabin on the table. They were very friendly, and if you weren't there on time they began their scolding. The blue jays waited noisily outside.

September 27, 1973

It was a temple in ruins, with its long roofless corridors, gates, headless statues and deserted courtyards. It had become a sanctuary for birds and monkeys, parrots and doves. Some of the headless statues were still massive in their beauty; they had a still dignity. The whole place was surprisingly clean, and one could sit on the ground to watch the monkeys and chattering birds. Once very long ago, the temple must have been a flourishing place with thousands of worshippers, with garlands, incense and prayer. Their atmosphere was still there, their hopes, fears and their reverence. The holy sanctuary was gone long ago. Now the monkeys disappeared as it was growing hot, but the parrots and doves had their nests in the holes and crevices of the high walls. This old ruined temple was too far away for the villagers to further destroy it. Had they come they would have desecrated the emptiness.

Religion has become superstition and image-worship, belief and ritual. It has lost the beauty of truth; incense has taken the place of reality. Instead of direct perception, there is in its place the image carved by the hand or the mind. The only concern of religion is the total transformation of man. And all the circus that goes on around it is nonsense. That is why truth is not to be found in any temple, church or mosque, however beautiful they are. The beauty of truth and the beauty of stone are two different things. One opens the door to the immeasurable, the other to the

43

imprisonment of man; one to freedom and the other to the bondage of thought. Romanticism and sentimentality deny the very nature of religion, nor is it a plaything of the intellect. Knowledge in the area of action is necessary to function efficiently and objectively, but knowledge is not the means of the transformation of man. Knowledge is the structure of thought, and thought is the dull repetition of the known, however modified and enlarged. There is no freedom through the ways of thought and the known.

The long snake lay very still along the dry ridge of the rice fields, lusciously green and bright in the morning sun. Probably it was resting or waiting for a careless frog. Frogs were then being shipped to Europe to be eaten as a delicacy. The snake was long and yellowish and very still; it was almost the colour of the dry earth, hard to see, but the light of day was in its dark eyes. The only thing that was moving, in and out, was its black tongue. It could not have been aware of the watcher who was somewhat behind its head.

Death was everywhere that morning. You could hear it in the village; the great sobs as the body, wrapped in a cloth, was being carried out; a kite was streaking down on a bird; an animal was being killed; you heard its agonising cries. So it went on day after day: death is always everywhere, as sorrow is.

The beauty of truth and its subtleties are not in belief and dogma; it is never where man can find them for there is no path to its beauty; it is not a fixed point, a haven of shelter. It has its own tenderness whose love is not to be measured, nor can you hold it, experience it. It has no market value to be used and put aside. It is there when the mind and heart are empty of the things of thought. The monk or the poor man are not near it, nor the rich; neither the intellectual nor the gifted can touch it. The one who says he knows has never come near it. Be far away from the world and yet live in it.

The parrots were screeching and fluttering around the tamarind tree that morning; they begin their restless activity early, with their coming and going. They were bright streaks of green with strong, red, curved beaks. They never seemed to fly straight but always zigzagging, shrieking as they flew. Occasionally they would come to sit on the parapet of the veranda; then you could watch them, but not for long; they would be off again with their crazy and noisy flight. Their only enemy seemed to be man. He puts them in a cage.

September 28, 1973

The big black dog had just killed a goat; it had been punished severely and tied up, and was now whining and barking. The house had a high wall around it, but somehow the goat had wandered in, and the dog had chased and killed it. The owner of the house made amends with words and silver. It was a large house with trees around it, and the lawn was never completely green however much it was watered. The sun was cruelly strong, and the flowers and bushes had to be watered twice a day. The soil was poor, and the heat of the day almost withered the greenery. But the trees had grown large and gave comforting shadows, and you could sit there in the early morning when the sun was well behind the trees. It was a good place if you wanted to sit quietly and lose yourself in meditation, but not if you wanted to daydream or lose yourself in some satisfying illusion. It was too severe there in those shadows, too demanding, for the whole place was given over to that kind of quiet contemplation. You could indulge in your friendly fantasies, but you would soon find out that the place did not invite the images of thought.

He was sitting with a cloth over his head, weeping; his wife had just died. He did not want to show his tears to his children; they too were crying, not quite understanding what had happened. The mother of many children had been unwell and lately very ill; now the father sat at her bedside. He never seemed to go out, and one day, after some ceremonies, the mother was carried out. The house had strangely become empty without the perfume that the mother had given to it, and it was never the same again for there was sorrow in the house now. The father knew it; the children had lost someone forever, but as yet they did not know the meaning of sorrow.

It is always there; you cannot just forget it; you cannot cover it up through some form of entertainment, religious or otherwise. You may run away from it, but it will be there to meet you again. You may lose yourself in worship, prayer or some comforting belief, but it will appear again, unbidden. The flowering of sorrow is bitterness, cynicism or some neurotic behaviour. You may be aggressive, violent and nasty in your conduct, but sorrow is where you are. You may have power, position and the pleasures of money, but it will be there in your heart, waiting and preparing. Do what you will, you cannot escape from it. The love that you have ends in sorrow; sorrow is time, sorrow is thought.

The tree is cut down, and you shed a tear; an animal is killed for your taste; the earth is being destroyed for your pleasure; you are being educated to kill, to destroy, man against man. New technology and machines are taking over the toils of man, but you may not end sorrow through the things that thought has put together. Love is not pleasure.

She came, desperate in her sorrow. She talked, pouring
out all the things she had been through: death, the
inanities of her children, their politics, their divorces, their
frustrations, bitterness and the utter futility of life that had
no meaning. She was not young anymore; in her youth,
she had enjoyed herself, had a passing interest in politics, a
degree in economics, and more or less the kind of life that
almost everyone leads. Her husband had died recently, and
all sorrow seemed to descend upon her. She became quiet
as we talked.

Any movement of thought is the deepening of sorrow.
Thought with its memories, with its images of pleasure
and pain, with its loneliness and tears, with its self-pity
and remorse, is the ground of sorrow. Listen to what is
being said. Just listen—not to the echoes of the past,
to the overcoming of sorrow or how to escape from its
torture—but listen with your heart, with your whole
being to what is now being said. Your dependence and
attachment have prepared the soil for your sorrow.
Your neglect of the study of yourself and the beauty it
brings has given nourishment to your sorrow; all your
self-centred activities have led you to this. Just listen to
what is being said: stay with it, don't wander off. Any
movement of thought is the strengthening of sorrow.
Thought is not love. Love has no sorrow.

September 29, 1973

The rains were nearly over, and the horizon was flowing with billowing white and golden clouds; they were soaring up to the blue and green heavens. The leaves of every bush were washed clean, and they were sparkling in the early morning sun. It was a morning of delight, the earth was rejoicing and there seemed to be benediction in the air. High up in that room you saw the blue sea, the river running into it, the palms and the mangoes. You held your breath at the wonder of the earth and the immense shape of the clouds. It was early, quiet, and the noise of the day had not yet begun; across the bridge, there was hardly any traffic, only a long line of bullock carts, laden with hay. Years later, buses would come with their pollution and bustle. It was a lovely morning, full of song and bliss.

The two brothers were driven in a car to a village nearby to see their father whom they had not seen for 15 years or more. They had to walk a little distance on an ill-kept road. They came to a storage of water; all its sides had stone steps leading down to the clear water. At one end of it was a small temple with a square tower, quite narrow at the top; there were many images in stone all around it. On the veranda of the temple, overlooking the big pond, were some people, absolutely still, like those images on the tower, lost in meditation. Beyond the water, just behind some other houses, was the house where the father lived.

He came out as the two brothers approached, and they greeted him by prostrating fully, touching his feet. They were shy and waited for him to speak, as was the custom.

Before he said anything, he went inside to wash his feet as the boys had touched them. He was a very orthodox Brahmin; no one could touch him except another Brahmin, and his two sons had been polluted by mixing with others who were not of his class and had eaten food cooked by non-Brahmins. So he washed his feet and sat down on the ground, not too close to his polluted sons. They talked for some time and the hour when food is eaten approached. He sent them away, for he could not eat with them; they were no longer Brahmins. He must have had affection for them, for, after all, they were his sons whom he had not seen for so many years. If their mother were alive, she might have given them food but certainly would not have eaten with her sons. They must have had a deep affection for their children, but orthodoxy and tradition forbade any physical contact with them. Tradition is very strong, stronger than love.

The tradition of war is stronger than love. The tradition of killing for food and killing the so-called enemy denies human tenderness and affection. The tradition of long hours of labour breeds efficient cruelty. The tradition of marriage soon becomes bondage. The traditions of the rich and the poor keep them apart. Each profession has its own tradition and its own elite, which breeds envy and enmity. The traditional ceremonies and rituals in the places of worship, the world over, have separated man from man, and the words and gestures have no meaning at all. A thousand yesterdays, however rich and beautiful, deny love.

You cross over a rickety bridge to the other side of a narrow, muddy stream which joins the big wide river. You come to a small village of mud and sun-dried bricks. There are quantities of children, screaming and playing; the older people are in the fields or fishing or working in the nearby town. In a small dark room, an opening in the wall is the window; no flies would come into this darkness. It was cool in there. In that small space was a weaver with a large loom; he could not read but was educated in his own way, polite and wholly absorbed in his labours. He turned out exquisite cloth of gold and silver with beautiful patterns. In whatever colour, he could weave traditional patterns, the finest and the best. He was born to that tradition; he was small, gentle and eager to show his marvellous talent. You watched him as he produced from silken threads the finest of cloths, with wonder and love in your heart. There was the woven piece of great beauty, born of long tradition.

September 30, 1973

A long yellowish snake was crossing the road under a banyan tree. He had been for a long walk and was coming back when he saw it. He followed it, quite closely, up a mound; it peered into every hole and was totally unaware of him, though he was almost on top of it. There was a large bulge in the middle of its length. The villagers on their way home had stopped talking and watched; one of them told him that it was a cobra and that he had better be careful. The cobra disappeared into a hole, and he resumed his walk. Intent on seeing the cobra again at the same spot, he returned the next day. There was no snake, but the villagers had put a shallow pot of milk, some marigolds and other flowers, and a large stone with some ashes on it. That place had become sacred, and every day there would be fresh flowers; the villagers all around knew that that place had become sacred. He returned several months later; there was fresh milk, fresh flowers and the stone was newly decorated. And the banyan was a little older.

The temple overlooked the Mediterranean. It was in ruins, and only the marble columns remained. In a war it was destroyed, but it was still a sacred sanctuary. One evening, with the golden sun on the marble, you felt the holy atmosphere; you were alone, with no visitors about and their endless chatter. The columns were becoming pure gold, and the sea far below was intensely blue. A statue of the goddess was there, preserved and locked up; you could only see her at certain hours, and she was losing the beauty of sacredness. The blue sea remained.

It was a nice cottage in the country, with a lawn that had been mown, rolled and weeded for many a year. The whole place was well looked after, prosperous and joyful. Behind the house was a small vegetable garden; it was a lovely place with a gentle stream running beside, making hardly a sound. The door opened and was held back by a statue of the Buddha, kicked into place. The owner was totally unaware of what he was doing; to him it was a doorstop. You wondered if he would do the same with a statue he revered, for he was a Christian. You deny the sacred things of another, but you keep your own. The beliefs of another are superstitions, but your own are reasonable and real. What is sacred?

On the beach, he had picked up a piece of sea-washed wood, in the shape of a human head. It was made of hardwood, shaped by the waters of the sea, cleansed by many seasons. He had brought it home and put it on the mantelpiece; he looked at it from time to time and admired what the sea had done. One day, he put some flowers around it and then it happened every day; he felt uncomfortable if there were not fresh flowers every day, and gradually that piece of shaped wood became very important in his life. He would allow no one to touch it except himself; they might desecrate it; he washed his hands before he touched it. It had become holy, sacred, and he alone was the high priest of it; he represented it; it told him of things he could never know by himself. His life was filled with it, and he was, he said, unspeakably happy.

What is sacred? Not the things made by the mind or hand or by the sea. The symbol is never the real; the word *grass* is not the grass of the field; the word *God* is not God. The word never contains the whole, however cunning the description. The word *sacred* has no meaning by itself; it becomes sacred only in its relationship to something, illusory or real. What is real is not the words of the mind; reality, truth, cannot be touched by thought. Where the perceiver is, truth is not. The thinker and his thought must come to an end for truth to be. Then that which is, is sacred—that ancient marble with the golden sun on it, that snake and the villager. Where there is no love, there is nothing sacred. Love is whole, and in it there is no fragmentation.

October 2, 1973

Consciousness is its content; the content is consciousness. All action is fragmentary when the content of consciousness is broken up. This activity breeds conflict, misery and confusion; then sorrow is inevitable.

From the air, at that height, you could see green fields, each separate from the other in shape, size and colour. A river came down to meet the sea; far beyond it were the mountains, heavy with snow. All over the earth, there were large, spreading towns and villages; on the hills were castles, churches and houses, and beyond them were the vast deserts, brown, golden and white. Then there was the blue sea again and more land with thick forests. The whole earth was rich and beautiful.

He walked there, hoping to meet a tiger, and he did. The villagers had come to tell his host that a tiger had killed a young cow the previous night and would come back that night to the kill. Would they like to see it? A platform on a tree would be built, and from there one could see the big killer. Also, they would tie a goat to the tree to make sure that the tiger would come. He said he wouldn't like to see a goat killed for his pleasure, so the matter was dropped. But late that afternoon, as the sun was behind a rolling hill, his host wished to go for a drive, hoping they might by chance see the tiger that had killed the cow. They drove for some miles into the forest; it became quite dark and with the headlights on they turned back. They had given up every hope of seeing the tiger as they drove back. But just as they turned a corner, there it was, sitting on its haunches in the middle of the road, huge, striped, its eyes bright in the headlamps. The car stopped and it came towards them growling, and the growls shook the car. It was surprisingly large and its long tail with a black tip was moving slowly from side to side. It was annoyed. The window was open, and as it passed growling, he put out his hand to stroke this great energy of the forest, but his host hurriedly snatched his arm back, explaining later that it would have torn his arm away. It was a magnificent animal, full of majesty and power.

Down there on that earth there were tyrants denying freedom to man, ideologists shaping the mind of man. Priests with their centuries of tradition and belief were enslaving man; the politicians with their endless promises were bringing corruption and division. Down there, man is caught in endless conflict and sorrow, and in the bright lights of pleasure. It is all so utterly meaningless—the pain, the labour and the words of philosophers. Death and unhappiness and toil, man against man.

This complex variety, modified changes in the pattern of pleasure and pain, is the content of man's consciousness, shaped and conditioned in the culture in which it has been nurtured, with its religious and economic pressures. Freedom is not within the boundaries of such a consciousness. What is accepted as freedom is, in reality, a prison made somewhat liveable in through the growth of technology. In this prison there are wars, made more destructive by science and profit. Freedom doesn't lie in the change of prisons, nor in any change of gurus, with their absurd authority. Authority does not bring the sanity of order. On the contrary, it breeds disorder, and out of this soil grows authority. Freedom is not in fragments. A non-fragmented mind, a mind that is whole is in freedom. It does not know it is free; what is known is within the area of time, the past through the present to the future. All movement is time and time is not a factor of freedom. Freedom of choice denies freedom; choice only exists where there is confusion. Clarity of perception, insight, is the freedom from the pain of choice. Total order is the light of freedom. This order is not the child of thought, for all activity of thought is to cultivate fragmentation. Love is not a fragment of thought or pleasure. The perception of this is intelligence. Love and intelligence are inseparable, and from this flows action which does not breed pain. Order is its ground.

October 3, 1973

It was quite cold at the airport so early in the morning; the sun was just coming up. Everyone was wrapped up, and the poor porters were shivering. There was the usual noise of an airport, the roars of the jets, the loud chatter, the farewells and the take-off. The plane was crowded with tourists, businessmen and others going to the holy city, with its filth and teeming people. Presently the vast range of the Himalayas became pink in the morning sun; we were flying southeast, and for hundreds of miles these immense peaks seemed to be hanging in the air with beauty and majesty. The passenger in the next seat was immersed in a newspaper; there was a woman across the aisle who was concentrating on her rosary; the tourists were talking loudly and taking photographs of each other and of the distant mountains; everyone was busy with their things and had no time to observe the marvel of the earth and its meandering sacred river, nor the subtle beauty of those great peaks which were becoming rose-coloured.

There was a man further down the aisle to whom considerable respect was being paid. He was not young, seemed to have the face of a scholar, was quick in movement, and cleanly dressed. One wondered if he ever saw the actual glory of those mountains. Presently he got up and came towards the passenger in the next seat; he asked if he might change places with him. He sat down, introducing himself, and asked if he might have a talk with us. He spoke English rather hesitantly, choosing his words carefully for he was not too familiar with this language; he had a clear, soft voice and was pleasant in his manners. He began by saying he was most fortunate to be travelling on the same plane and to have this conversation. 'Of course, I have heard of you since my youth and only the other day I heard your last talk: meditation and the observer. I am a scholar, a pundit, practising my own kind of meditation and discipline.'

The mountains were receding further east, and below us the river was making wide and friendly patterns.

'You said the observer is the observed, the meditator is the meditation and there is meditation only when the observer is not. I would like to be informed about this. For me, meditation has been the control of thought, fixing the mind on the absolute.'

The controller is the controlled, is it not? The thinker is his thoughts. Without words, images and thoughts, is there a thinker? The experiencer is the experience; without experience there is no experiencer. The controller of thought is made up of thought; he is one of the fragments of thought. Call it what you will, the outside agency, however sublime, is still a product of thought. The activity of thought is always outward and brings about fragmentation.

'Can life ever be lived without control? It is the essence of discipline.'

When the controller is the controlled, seen as an absolute fact, as truth, there comes about a totally different kind of energy which transforms *what is*. The controller can never change *what is*; he can control it, suppress it, modify it or run away from it, but can never go beyond and above it. Life can and must be lived without control. A controlled life is never sane; it breeds endless conflict, misery and confusion.

'This is a totally new concept.'

If it may be pointed out, it is not an abstraction, a formula. There is only *what is*. Sorrow is not an abstraction; one can draw a conclusion from it, a concept, a verbal structure, but it is not *what is*, sorrow. Ideologies have no reality; there is only *what is*. This can never be transformed when the observer separates himself from the observed.

'Is this your direct experience?'

It would be utterly vain and stupid if this were merely verbal structures of thought. To talk of such things would be hypocrisy.

'I would have liked to find out from you what meditation is, but now there is no time as we are about to land.'

There were garlands on arrival, and the winter sky was intensely blue.

October 4, 1973

As a young boy, he used to sit by himself under a large tree near a pond in which lotuses grew; they were pink and had a strong smell. From the shade of that spacious tree, he would watch the thin green snakes and the chameleons, the frogs and the water snakes. His brother, with others, would come to take him home.

It was a pleasant place under the tree, with the river and the pond. There seemed to be so much space, and in this the tree made its own space. Everything needs space. All those birds on telegraph wires, sitting so equally spaced on a quiet evening, make the space for the heavens.

The two brothers would sit with many others in the room with pictures; there would be a chant in Sanskrit and then complete silence. It was the evening meditation. The younger brother would go to sleep and roll over and wake up only when the others got up to leave. The room was not too large and within its walls were the pictures, the images of the sacred. Within the narrow confines of a temple or church, man gives form to the vast movement of space. It is like this everywhere; in the mosque, it is held in the graceful lines of words. Love needs great space.

To that pond would come snakes and occasionally people; it had stone steps leading down to the water where grew the lotus. The space that thought creates is measurable, and so is limited; cultures and religions are its product. But the mind is filled with thought and is made up of thought. Its consciousness is the structure of thought, having little space within it. But this space is the movement of time, from here to there, from its centre towards its outer lines of consciousness, narrow or expanding. The space which the centre makes for itself is its own prison. Its relationships are from this narrow space, but there must be space to live; that of the mind denies living. Living within the narrow confines of the centre is strife, pain and sorrow, and that is not living.

The space, the distance between you and the tree, is the word and knowledge, which is time. Time is the observer who makes the distance between himself and the trees, between himself and *what is*. Without the observer, distance ceases. Identification with trees, with another or with a formula, is the action of thought in its desire for protection, security. Distance is from one point to another and to reach that point, time is necessary; distance only exists where there is direction, inward or outward. The observer makes a separation, a distance between himself and *what is*; from this grows conflict and sorrow. The transformation of *what is* takes place only when there is no separation, no time, between the seer and the seen. Love has no distance.

The brother died, and there was no movement in any direction away from sorrow. This non-movement is the ending of time. It was among the hills and green shadows that the river began, and with a roar it entered the sea and the endless horizons. Man lives in boxes with drawers, acres of them, and they have no space; they are violent, brutal, aggressive and mischievous; they separate and destroy each other. The river is the earth and the earth is the river; each cannot exist without the other.

There are no ends to words, but communication is verbal and non-verbal. The hearing of the word is one thing and the hearing of no word is another; the one is irrelevant, superficial, leading to inaction; the other is non-fragmentary action, the flowering of goodness. Words have given beautiful walls but no space. Remembrance, imagination, are the pain of pleasure, and love is not pleasure.

The long, thin, green snake was there that morning; it was delicate and almost lost among the green leaves; it would be there, motionless, waiting and watching. The large head of the chameleon was showing; it lay along a branch; it changed its colour quite often.

October 6, 1973

There is a single tree in a green field that occupies a whole
acre; it is old and highly respected by all the other trees on
the hill. In its solitude, it dominates the noisy stream, the
hills and the cottage across the wooden bridge. You admire
it as you pass it by, but on your return you look at it in a
more leisurely way; its trunk is very large, deeply embedded
in the earth, solid and indestructible; its branches are long,
dark and curving; it has rich shadows. In the evening
it is withdrawn into itself, unapproachable, but during
the daylight hours it is open and welcoming. It is whole,
untouched by axe or saw. On a sunny day, you sat under it
and felt its venerable age, and because you were alone with
it you were aware of the depth and the beauty of life.

The old villager wearily passed you by, as you were
sitting on a bridge looking at the sunset; he was almost
blind, limping, carrying a bundle in one hand and in the
other a stick. It was one of those evenings when the colours
of the sunset were on every rock, tree and bush; the grass
and the fields seemed to have their own inner light. The
sun had set behind a hill, and amidst these extravagant
colours was the birth of the evening star. The villager
stopped in front of you and looked at those startling
colours and at you. You looked at each other, and without
a word he trudged on. In that communication there was
affection, tenderness and respect, not the silly respect but

that of religious men. At that moment all time and thought
had come to an end. You and he were utterly religious,
uncorrupted by belief or image, by word or poverty. You
often passed each other on that road among the stony hills
and each time, as you looked at one another, there was the
joy of total insight.

A man and his wife were coming from the temple
across the way. They were both silent, deeply stirred by
the chants and the worship. You happened to be walking
behind them, and you caught the feeling of their reverence,
the strength of their determination to lead a religious life.
But it would soon pass away as they were drawn into their
responsibility to their children, who came rushing towards
them. He had some kind of profession, was probably
capable, for he had a large house. The weight of existence
would drown him, and although he would go to the temple
often, the battle would go on.

The word is not the thing; the image, the symbol is not
the real. Reality, truth, is not a word. To put it into words
wipes it away and illusion takes its place. The intellect
may reject the whole structure of ideology, belief and all
the trappings and power that go with them, but reason
can justify any belief, any ideation. Reason is the order of
thought, and thought is the response of the outer. Because
it is the outer, thought puts together the inner. No man
can ever live only with the outer, and the inner becomes a

necessity. This division is the ground on which the battle of *me* and *not me* takes place. The outer is the god of religions and ideologies; the inner tries to conform to those images and conflict ensues.

There is neither the outer nor the inner but only the whole. The experiencer is the experienced. Fragmentation is insanity. This wholeness is not merely a word; it is when the division as the outer and inner utterly ceases. The thinker is the thought.

Suddenly, as you are walking along, without a single thought but only observing without the observer, you become aware of a sacredness that thought has never been able to conceive. You stop, you observe the trees, the birds and the passer-by; it is not an illusion or something with which the mind deludes itself. It is there in your eyes, in your whole being. The colour of the butterfly is the butterfly.

The colours which the sun had left were fading, and before dark the shy new moon showed itself before it disappeared behind the hill.

October 7, 1973

It was one of those mountain rains that lasts three or four days, bringing with it cooler weather. The earth was sodden and heavy, and all the mountain paths were slippery; small streams were running down the steep slopes, and labour in the terraced fields had stopped. The trees and the tea plantations were weary of the dampness; there had been no sun for over a week, and it was getting chilly. The mountains lay to the north, with their snow and gigantic peaks. The flags around the temples were heavy with rain; they had lost their delight, their gay colours fluttering in the breeze. There was thunder and lightning, and the sound carried from valley to valley; a thick fog hid the sharp flashes of light.

The next morning there was the clear, blue, tender sky, and the great peaks, still and timeless, were alight with the early morning sun. A deep valley ran down between the village and the high mountains; it was filled with dark blue fog. Straight ahead, towering in the clear sky was the second highest peak of the Himalayas. You could almost touch it, but it was many miles away; you forgot the distance for it was there, in all its majesty, so utterly pure and measureless. By late morning it was gone, hidden in the darkening clouds from the valley. Only in the early morning it showed itself and disappeared a few hours later. No wonder the ancients looked to their gods in these

mountains, in thunder and the clouds. The divinity of
their life was in the benediction that lay hidden in these
unapproachable snows.

His disciples came to invite you to visit their guru.
You politely refused, but they often came, hoping that
you would change your mind or accept their invitation,
becoming weary of their insistence. So it was decided that
their guru would come with a few of his chosen disciples.

It was a noisy little street; the children played cricket
there; they had a bat, and the stumps were a few odd bricks.
With shouts and laughter, they played cheerfully as long
as they could, only stopping for a passing car as the driver
respected their play. They would play day after day, and
that morning they were particularly noisy when the guru
came. He carried a small, polished stick.

Several of us were sitting on a thin mattress on the floor
when he entered the room, and we got up and offered him
the mattress. He sat cross-legged, putting his cane in front
of him; that thin mattress seemed to give him a position
of authority. He had found truth, experienced it and so
he, who knew, was opening the door for us. What he
said was law to him and others; you were merely a seeker,
whereas he had found. You might be lost in your search,
and he would help you along the way, but you must obey.
Quietly you replied that all seeking and finding had no

meaning unless the mind was free from its conditioning; that freedom is the first and last step, and obedience to any authority in matters of the mind is to be caught in illusion and action that breeds sorrow. He looked at you with pity and concern, and with a flare of annoyance, as though you were slightly demented. Then he said, 'The greatest and final experience has been given to me, and no seeker can refuse that.'

If reality or truth is to be experienced, it is only a projection of your own mind. What is experienced is not truth but a creation of your own mind.

His disciples were getting fidgety. Followers destroy their teachers and themselves. He got up and left, followed by his disciples. The children were still playing in the street; somebody was bowled out, followed by wild clapping and cheers.

There is no path to truth, historically or religiously. It is not to be experienced or found through dialectics; it is not to be seen in shifting opinions and beliefs. You will come upon it when the mind is free of all the things it has put together. That majestic peak is also the miracle of life.

October 8, 1973

The monkeys were all over the place that quiet morning; on the veranda, on the roof and in the mango tree—a whole troop of them. They were the brownish red-faced variety. The little ones were chasing each other among the trees, not too far from their mothers, and the big male was sitting by himself, keeping an eye over the whole troop; there must have been about twenty of them. They were rather destructive. As the sun rose higher, they slowly disappeared into the deeper wood, away from human habitation; the male was the first to leave and the others followed quietly. Then the parrots and crows came back with their usual clatter announcing their presence. There was a crow that would call, or whatever it does, in a raucous voice, usually about the same time, and keep it up until it was chased away. Day after day, it would repeat this performance; its caw penetrated deeply into the room and somehow all other noises seemed to have come to an end. These crows prevent violent quarrels amongst themselves, are quick, very watchful and efficient in their survival. The monkeys don't seem to like them. It was going to be a nice day.

He was a thin, wiry man, with a well-shaped head and eyes that had known laughter. We were sitting on a bench overlooking the river in the shade of a tamarind tree, the home of many parrots and a pair of small screech owls which were sunning themselves in the early morning sun.

He said, 'I have spent many years in meditation, controlling my thoughts, fasting and having only one meal a day. I used to be a social worker, but I gave it up long ago as I found such work did not solve the deep human problem. There are many others who are carrying on with this work, but it is no longer for me. It has become important for me to understand the full meaning and depth of meditation. Every school of meditation advocates some form of control; I have practised different systems, but somehow there seems to be no end to it.'

Control implies division, the controller and the thing to be controlled. This division, as all division, brings about conflict and distortion in action and behaviour. This fragmentation is the work of thought, one fragment trying to control the other parts; call this one fragment the controller or whatever name you will. This division is artificial and mischievous. Actually, the controller is the controlled. Thought in its very nature is fragmentary, and this causes confusion and sorrow. Thought has divided the world into nationalities, ideologies and religious sects, the big ones and the little ones. Thought is the response of memories, experience and knowledge, stored up in the brain; it can only function efficiently, sanely, when it has security, order. To survive physically, it must protect itself from all dangers. The necessity of outward survival is easy to understand, but the psychological survival is quite another matter, the survival of the image that thought has put together. Thought has divided existence as the outer and the inner, and from this separation conflict and control arise. For the survival of the inner, belief, ideology, gods, nationalities, conclusions become essential, and this also brings about untold wars, violence and sorrow. The desire for the survival of the inner, with its many images, is a disease, is disharmony. Thought is disharmony. All its images, ideologies, its truths are self-contradictory and destructive. Thought has brought about, apart from its technological achievements, both outwardly and inwardly, chaos and pleasures that soon become agonies.

To read all this in your daily life, to hear and see the movement of thought is the transformation that meditation brings about. This transformation is not the *me* becoming the greater *me* but the transformation of the content of consciousness. Consciousness is its content. The consciousness of the world is your consciousness; you are the world and the world is you. Meditation is the complete transformation of thought and its activities. Harmony is not the fruit of thought; it comes with the perception of the whole.

The morning breeze had gone and not a leaf was stirring. The river had become utterly still and the noises on the other bank came across the wide waters. Even the parrots were quiet.

October 9, 1973

You went by a narrow-gauge train that stopped at almost
every station where vendors of hot coffee and tea, blankets
and fruit, sweets and toys, were shouting their wares. Sleep
was almost impossible. In the morning, the passengers
got into a boat that crossed the shallow waters of the sea
to the island. There a train was waiting to take you to the
capital, through green country of jungles and palms, tea
plantations and villages. It was a pleasant and happy land.
By the sea it was hot and humid, but in the hills, where the
tea plantations were, it was cool. In the air was the smell of
ancient days, uncrowded and simple. But in the city, as in
all cities, there was noise, dirt, the squalor of poverty and
the vulgarity of money; in the harbour were ships from all
over the world.

The house was in a secluded part of the city, and there
was a constant flow of people who came to greet him with
garlands and fruit. One day, a man asked if he would like
to see a baby elephant, and naturally we went to see it. It
was about two weeks old, and its mother was nervous and
very protective, we were told. The car took us out of town,
past the squalor and dirt to a river with brown water, with
a village on its bank, tall and heavy trees surrounded it.
The elephant and the baby were there. He stayed there for
several hours until the mother got used to him; he had to
be introduced, was allowed to touch its long trunk and to

feed her some fruit and sugar cane. The sensitive end of the trunk was asking for more, and apples and bananas went into her wide mouth. The newly born baby was standing, waving her tiny trunk, between her mother's legs. She was a small replica of her huge mother. At last, the mother allowed him to touch her baby; its skin was not too rough, and its trunk was constantly on the move, much more alive than the rest of it. The mother was watching all the time, and her keeper had to reassure her from time to time. It was a playful baby.

A woman came into the small room deeply distressed. Her son was killed in the war: 'I loved him very much, and he was my only child. He was well-educated and had the promise of great goodness and talent. He was killed, and why should it happen to him and to me? There was real affection, love between us. It was such a cruel thing to happen.' She was sobbing and there seemed to be no end to her tears. She took his hand, and presently became quiet enough to listen.

We spend so much money on educating our children; we give them so much care; we become deeply attached to them; they fill our lonely lives; in them we find our fulfilment, our sense of continuity. Why are we educated? To become technological machines? To spend our days in labour and die in an accident or with a painful disease? This is the life that our culture and religion have brought us. Wives and mothers are crying all over the world; war or disease have claimed the husbands and sons. Is love attachment? Is love tears and the agony of loss? Is it loneliness and sorrow? Is it self-pity and the pain of separation? If you loved your son, you would see to it that no son was ever killed in a war. There have been thousands of wars, and mothers and wives have never totally denied the ways that lead to war. You will cry in agony, and support, unwillingly, the systems that breed war. Love knows no violence.

A man explained why he was separating from his wife. 'We married quite young, and after a few years things began to go wrong in every way, sexually, mentally, and we seemed so utterly unsuited to each other. We loved each other, though, at the beginning and gradually it is turning into hate; separation has become necessary, and the lawyers are seeing to it.'

Is love pleasure and the insistence of desire? Is love physical sensation? Are attraction and its fulfilment love? Is it a commodity of thought? A thing put together by an accident of circumstances? Is it of companionship, kindliness and friendship? If any of these take precedence, then it is not love. Love is as final as death.

There is a path that goes into the high mountains through woods, meadows and open spaces. And there is a bench before the climb begins and on it an old couple sit, looking down on the sunlit valley. They come there very often and sit without a word, silently watching the beauty of the earth. They are waiting for death to come. And the path goes on into the snows.

October 10, 1973

The rains had come and gone, and the huge boulders were glistening in the morning sun. There was water in the riverbeds, and the land was rejoicing once again; the earth was redder, every bush and blade of grass was greener, and the deep-rooted trees were putting out new leaves. The cattle were getting fatter and the villagers less thin. These hills are as old as the earth, and the huge boulders appear to have been carefully balanced there. There is a hill towards the east that has the shape of a great platform, on which a square temple has been constructed. The village children walked several miles to learn to read and write; there was one small child, all by herself, with a shining face, going to school in the next village, a book in one hand and some food in the other. She stopped as we went by, shy and inquisitive; if she stayed longer, she would be late for school. The rice fields were startlingly green. It was a long, peaceful morning.

Two crows were squabbling in the air, cawing and tearing at each other; there was not enough foothold in the air, so they came down to the earth, struggling with each other. On the ground, feathers began to fly and the fight began to be serious. Suddenly about a dozen other crows descended upon them and put an end to their fight. After a lot of cawing and scolding, they all disappeared into the trees.

Violence is everywhere, among the highly educated and the most primitive, among the intellectuals and the sentimentalists. Neither education nor organised religions have been able to tame man; on the contrary, they have been responsible for wars, tortures, concentration camps and the slaughter of animals on land and sea. The more he progresses, the crueller man seems to become. Politics has become gangsterism, one group against another; nationalism has led to war; there are economic wars; there are personal hatreds and violence. Man doesn't seem to learn from experience and knowledge, and violence in every form goes on. What place has knowledge in the transformation of man and society?

The energy that has gone into the accumulation of knowledge has not changed man; it has not put an end to violence. The energy that has gone into a thousand explanations of why we are so aggressive, brutal, insensitive, has not put an end to our cruelty. The energy which has been spent in analysis of the causes of our insane destruction, our pleasure in violence, sadism, the bullying activity, has in no way made man considerate and gentle. In spite of all the words and books, threats and punishments, man continues in violence.

Violence is not only in the killing, in the bomb, in revolutionary change through bloodshed; it is deeper and more subtle. Conformity and imitation are the indications

of violence; imposition and the accepting of authority
are an indication of violence; ambition and competition
are an expression of this aggression and cruelty, and
comparison breeds envy with its animosity and hatred.
Where there is conflict, inner or outer, there is the ground
for violence. Division in all its forms brings about conflict
and pain.

You know all this; you have read about the actions of
violence, you have seen it in yourself and around you,
and you have heard it. You have knowledge of all this and
perhaps more, and yet violence has not come to an end.
Why? The explanations and the causes of such behaviour
have no real significance. If you are indulging in them,
you are wasting your energy which you need to transcend
violence. You need all your energy to meet and go beyond
the energy that is being wasted in violence. Controlling
violence is another form of violence, for the controller is the
controlled. In total attention, the summation of all energy,
violence in all its forms comes to an end. Attention is not
a word, an abstract formula of thought, but an act in daily
life. Action is not an ideology, but if action is the outcome
of it, then it leads to violence.

After the rains, the river goes around every boulder,
through towns and villages, and however much it is
polluted, it cleanses itself and runs through valleys, gorges
and meadows.

October 12, 1973

Again a well-known guru came to see him. We sat in a lovely walled garden; the lawn was green and well kept. There were roses, sweet peas, bright yellow marigolds and other flowers of the oriental north. The wall and the trees kept out the noise of the few cars that went by; the air carried the perfume of many flowers. In the evening, a family of jackals would come out from their hiding place under a tree; they had scratched out a large hole where the mother had her three cubs. They were a healthy-looking lot and soon after sunset the mother would come out with them, keeping close to the trees. Garbage was behind the house, and they would look for it later. There was also a family of mongooses. Every evening the mother with her pink nose and her long fat tail would come out from her hiding place followed by her two kits, one behind the other, keeping close to the wall. They too came to the back of the kitchen where sometimes things were left for them. They kept the garden free of snakes. They and the jackals seemed never to have crossed each other, but if they did, they left each other alone.

The guru had announced a few days before that he wished to pay a call. He arrived, and his disciples came streaming in afterwards, one by one. They would touch his feet as a mark of great respect. They wanted to touch the other man's feet too, but he would not have it; he told them it was degrading,

but tradition and hope of heaven were too strong in them.
The guru would not enter the house as he had taken a
vow never to enter a house of married people. The sky was
intensely blue that morning, and the shadows were long.

'You deny being a guru, but you are a guru of gurus.
I have observed you from your youth and what you say
is the truth, which few will understand. For the many we
are necessary; otherwise they would be lost. Our authority
saves the foolish. We are the interpreters. We have had our
experiences; *we know*. Tradition is a rampart, and only the
very few can stand alone and see the naked reality. You are
among the blessed, but we must walk with the crowd, sing
their songs, repeat the holy names and sprinkle holy water,
which does not mean that we are entirely hypocrites. They
need help, and we are there to give it. What, if one may be
allowed to ask, is the experience of that absolute reality?'

The disciples were still coming and going, uninterested
in the conversation and indifferent to their surroundings,
to the beauty of the flower and the tree. A few of them
were sitting on the grass listening, hoping not to be too
disturbed. A cultured man is discontented with his culture.

Reality is not to be experienced. There is no path to it,
and no word can indicate it; it is not to be sought after and
be found. The finding, after seeking, is the corruption of
the mind. The very word *truth* is not truth; the description
is not the described.

'The ancients have told of their experiences, their bliss in meditation, their superconsciousness, their holy reality. If one may be allowed to ask, must one set aside all this and their exalted example?'

Any authority on meditation is the very denial of it. All the knowledge, concepts and examples have no place in meditation. The complete elimination of the meditator, the experiencer, the thinker, is the very essence of meditation. This freedom is the daily act of meditation. The observer is the past; his ground is time. His thoughts, images, shadows, are time-binding. Knowledge is time, and freedom from the known is the flowering of meditation. There is no system, and so there is no direction to truth or to the beauty of meditation. To follow another, their example, their word, is to banish truth. Only in the mirror of relationship do you see the face of *what is*. The seer is the seen. Without the order which virtue brings, meditation and the endless assertions of others have no meaning whatsoever; they are totally irrelevant. Truth has no tradition; it cannot be handed down.

In the sun, the smell of sweet peas was very strong.

October 13, 1973

We were flying smoothly at thirty-seven thousand feet, and the plane was full. We had passed the sea and were approaching land; far below us was the sea and land. The passengers never seemed to stop talking or drinking or flipping the pages of a magazine; then there was a film. They were a noisy group to be entertained and fed; they slept, snored and held hands. The land was soon covered over by masses of clouds from horizon to horizon, space and depth and the noise of chatter. Between the earth and the plane were endless white clouds and above was the gentle blue sky. In the corner seat by a window, you were widely awake watching the changing shape of the clouds and the white light upon them.

Has consciousness any depth or only a surface fluttering? Thought can imagine its depth, can assert that it has depth or only consider the surface ripples. Has thought itself any depth at all? Consciousness is made up of its content; its content is its entire frontier. Thought is the activity of the outer, and in certain languages thought means the outside. The importance that is given to the hidden layers of consciousness is still on the surface, without any depth. Thought can give to itself a centre, as the ego, the *me*, and that centre has no depth at all; words, however cunningly and subtly put together, are not profound. The *me* is a fabrication of thought in word and identification; the *me*, seeking depth in action, in existence, has no meaning at all; all its attempts to establish depth in relationship end in the multiplications of its own images, whose shadows it considers are deep. All the activities of thought have no depth; its pleasures, its fears, its sorrow are on the surface. The very word *surface* indicates that there is something below, a great volume of water or very shallow. A shallow or a deep mind are the words of thought and thought in itself is superficial. The volume behind thought is experience, knowledge, memory, things that are gone, only to be recalled, to be or not to be acted upon.

Far below us, down on the earth, a wide river was rolling along, with wide curves amid scattered farms, and on the winding roads were crawling ants. The mountains were covered with snow and the valleys were green with deep shadows. The sun was directly ahead and went down into the sea as the plane landed in the fumes and noise of an expanding city.

Is there depth to life, to existence at all? Is all relationship shallow? Can thought ever discover depth? Thought is the only instrument that man has cultivated and sharpened, and when that is denied as a means to the understanding of depth in life, the mind seeks other means. To lead a shallow life soon becomes wearying, boring, meaningless, and from this arises the constant pursuit of pleasure, with fears, conflict and violence. To see the fragments that thought has brought about and their activity, as a whole, is the ending of thought. Perception of the whole is only possible when the observer, who is one of the fragments of thought, is not active. Then action is relationship and never leads to conflict and sorrow.

Silence has depth, as love. Silence is not the movement of thought, nor is love. Only then the words *deep* and *shallow* lose their meaning. There is no measurement to love or to silence. What is measurable is thought and time. Thought is time. Measurement is necessary, but when thought carries it into action and relationship, then mischief and disorder begin. Order is not measurable, only disorder is.

The sea and the house were quiet. The hills behind them, with all the wildflowers of spring, were silent.

ROME

October 17, 1973

It had been a hot, dry summer with occasional showers;
the lawns were turning brown but the tall trees, with
their heavy foliage, were happy and the flowers were
blooming. The land had not seen such a summer for
years and the farmers were pleased. In the cities it was
dreadful: the polluted air, the heat and the crowded streets.
The chestnuts were already turning slightly brown, and
the parks were full of people, with children shouting
and running all over the place. In the country it was
very beautiful; there is always peace in the land, and the
narrow river with swans and ducks brought enchantment.
Romanticism and sentimentality were safely locked up
in the cities, and here, deep in the country, with trees,
meadows and streams, there was beauty and delight.

There is a road that goes through the woods and
dappled shadows, and every leaf holds that beauty,
every dying leaf and blade of grass. Beauty is not a

word, an emotional response; it is not soft, to be twisted and moulded by thought. When beauty is there, every movement and action in every form of relationship is whole, sane and holy. When that beauty and love doesn't exist, the world goes mad.

On the small screen, the preacher, with carefully cultivated gesture and word, was saying that he knew that his saviour, the only saviour, was living; if he were not living, there would be no hope for the world. The aggressive thrust of his arm drove away any doubt or inquiry, for he knew and you must stand up for what he knew, for his knowledge is your knowledge, your conviction. The calculated movement of his arms and the driven word were substance and encouragement to his audience, which was there with its mouth open, both young and old, spellbound and worshipping the image of their mind. A war had just begun, and neither the preacher nor his large audience cared, for wars must go on and besides it is part of their culture.

On that screen a little later, there was shown what the scientists were doing, their marvellous inventions, their extraordinary space control, the world of tomorrow, the new complex machines; the explanations of how cells are formed, the experiments that are being made on animals, on worms and flies. The study of the behaviour of animals was carefully and amusingly explained. With this study, professors could better understand human behaviour.

The remains of an ancient culture were explained; the excavations, the vases, the carefully preserved mosaics and the crumbling walls; the wonderful world of the past, its temples, its glories. Many, many volumes have been written about the riches, the paintings, the cruelties and the greatness of the past, its kings and its slaves.

A little later, the actual war that was raging in the desert was shown, and among the green hills were the enormous tanks and the low-flying jets, the noise and the calculated slaughter. The politicians were talking about peace but encouraging war in every land. The crying women were shown and the desperately wounded, the children waving flags and the priests intoning blessings.

The tears of humanity have not washed away our desire to kill. Religions have not stopped war; on the contrary, they have encouraged it, have blessed the weapons of war, have divided people. Governments are isolated and cherish their insularity. Scientists are supported by governments. The preacher is lost in his words and images.

You will cry, but educate your children to kill and be killed. You accept it as the way of life. Your commitment is to your own security; it is your god and your sorrow. You care for your children so carefully, so generously, but then you are so enthusiastically willing for them to be killed. They showed on the screen baby seals, with enormous eyes, being killed.

The function of culture is to transform man totally.

Across the river, mandarin ducks were splashing and chasing each other, and the shadows of the trees were on the water.

October 18, 1973

There is in Sanskrit a long prayer to peace. It was written many centuries ago by someone to whom peace was an absolute necessity, and perhaps his daily life had its roots in that. It was written before the creeping poison of nationalism, the immorality of the power of money, and the insistence on worldliness that industrialism has brought about. The prayer is to enduring peace: May there be peace among the gods, in heaven and among the stars. May there be peace on earth, among men and four-footed animals. May we not hurt each other. May we be generous to each other. May we have that intelligence which will guide our life and action. May there be peace in our prayer, on our lips and in our hearts.

There is no mention of individuality in this peace; that came much later. There is only ourselves—our peace, our intelligence, our knowledge, our enlightenment. The sound of Sanskrit chants seems to have a strange effect. In a temple, about fifty priests were chanting in Sanskrit, and the very walls seemed to be vibrating.

There is a path that goes through the green, shining field, through a sunlit wood and beyond. Hardly anyone comes to these woods, full of light and shadows. It is very peaceful there, quiet and isolated. There are squirrels and an occasional deer, shyly watchful and dashing away; the

squirrels watch you from a branch and sometimes scold
you. These woods have the perfume of summer and the
smell of damp earth. There are enormous trees, old and
moss-laden; they welcome you, and you feel the warmth of
their welcome. Each time you sit there and look up through
the branches and leaves at the wonderful blue sky, that
peace and welcome are waiting for you.

You went with others through the woods, but there were
aloofness and silence; people were chattering, indifferent
and unaware of the dignity and grandeur of the trees; they
had no relationship with them and so in all probability, no
relationship with each other. The relationship between the
trees and you was complete and immediate; they and you
were friends, and thus you were the friend of every tree,
bush and flower on earth. You were not there to destroy,
and there was peace between them and you.

Peace is not an interval between the ending and
beginning of a conflict, of pain and of sorrow. No
government can bring peace; its peace is of corruption and
decay. The orderly rule of a people breeds degeneration
for it is not concerned with all the people of the earth.
Tyrannies can never hold peace for they destroy freedom:
peace and freedom go together. To kill another for peace
is the idiocy of ideologies. You cannot buy peace; it is not
the invention of intellect; it is not to be purchased through
prayer, through bargaining. It is not in any holy building,

in any book, in any person. No one can lead you to it, no guru, no priest, no symbol.

In meditation it is. Meditation itself is the movement of peace. It is not an end to be found; it is not put together by thought or word. The action of meditation is intelligence. Meditation is none of those things you have been taught or experienced. The putting away of what you have learnt and experienced is meditation. The freedom from the experiencer is meditation. When there is no peace in relationship, there is no peace in meditation; it is an escape into illusion and fanciful dreams. It cannot be demonstrated or described. You are no judge of peace. You will be aware of it, if it is there, through the activities of your daily life, the order, the virtue of your life.

Heavy clouds and mists were there that morning; it was going to rain. It would take several days to see the blue sky again. But as you came into the wood, there was no diminishing of that peace and welcome. There was utter stillness and incomprehensible peace. The squirrels were hiding and the grasshoppers in the meadows were silent, and beyond the hills and valleys was the restless sea.

October 19, 1973

The wood was asleep; the path through it was dark and winding. There was not a thing stirring. The long twilight was disappearing and the silence of the night was covering the earth. The small gurgling stream, so insistent during the day, was conceding to the quietness of the coming night. Through the small opening among the leaves were the stars, brilliant and very close. The darkness of the night is as necessary as the light of day. The welcoming trees were withdrawn into themselves and distant; they were all around, but were aloof and unapproachable; they were asleep, not to be disturbed. In this quiet darkness, there was growth and flowering, gathering strength to meet the vibrant day. Night and day are essential; both give life, energy, to all living things. Only man dissipates it.

Sleep is very important, a sleep without too many dreams, without tossing about too much. In sleep, many things happen in the physical organism, in the brain; the mind is the brain, the heart and the organism; they are all one, a unitary movement. To this whole structure, sleep is also absolutely essential. In sleep, order, adjustment, and deeper perceptions take place. The quieter the brain, the deeper is the insight. The brain needs security and order to function harmoniously, without any friction. The night provides it, and during quiet sleep there are movements, states, which thought can never reach. Dreams are disturbance; they distort total perception. In sleep the mind rejuvenates itself.

You might say dreams are necessary; that if one doesn't dream, one might go mad; they are helpful, revealing. There are superficial dreams, without much meaning; there are dreams that are significant, and there is also a dreamless state. Dreams are the expression in different forms and symbols of our daily life. If there is no harmony, no order in our daily life of relationship, then dreams are a continuance of that disorder. The brain during sleep tries to bring about order out of this confusing contradiction. In this constant struggle between order and disorder, the brain is worn out. But it must have security and order to function at all, and so beliefs, ideologies and other neurotic concepts become necessary. Turning night into day is one of those neurotic habits; the inanities that go on in the modern world after nightfall are an escape from the daytime of routine and boredom.

The total awareness of disorder in relationship both private and public, personal and distant, an awareness of *what is* without any choice during conscious hours during the day, brings order out of disorder. Then the brain has no need to seek order during sleep. Then dreams are only superficial, without meaning. Order in the whole of consciousness, not merely at the conscious level, takes place when division between the observer and the observed ceases completely. *What is* is transcended when the observer who is the past, who is time, comes to an end. The active present, the *what is*, is not in the bondage of time as the observer is.

During sleep, when the mind—the brain and the organism—has this total order, then only is there an awareness of that wordless state, that timeless movement. This is not some fanciful dream, an abstraction of escape. It is the very summation of meditation. That is, the brain is active, waking or sleeping, but the constant conflict between order and disorder wears it down. Order is the highest form of virtue, sensitivity and intelligence. When there is this great beauty of order and harmony, the brain is not endlessly active. Certain parts of it have to carry the burden of memory, but that is a very small part; the rest of the brain is free from the noise of experience. That freedom is the order and harmony of silence. This freedom and the noise of memory move together; intelligence is the action of this movement. Meditation is the freedom from the known and yet operating in the field of the known. There is no *me* as the operator. In sleep or awake, this meditation goes on.

The path came slowly out of the woods and from horizon to horizon the sky was filled with stars. In the fields, not a thing moved.

October 20, 1973

It is the oldest living thing on the earth. It is gigantic in proportion, with its height and vast trunk. Among other redwood trees, which were also very old, this one was towering over them all; other trees had been touched by fire, but this one had no marks on it. It had lived through the ugly things of history, through the wars of the world, through the mischief and sorrow of man, through fire and lightning, through the storms of time, untouched, majestic and utterly alone, with immense dignity. There had been fires, but the bark of these redwood trees was able to resist them and survive.

The noisy tourists had not yet come and you could be alone with this great silent one. It soared up to the heavens as you sat under it, vast and timeless. Its very years gave it the dignity of silence and the aloofness of great age. It was as silent as your mind was, as still as your heart, and living without the burden of time. You were aware of compassion that time had never touched and of innocence that had never known hurt and sorrow. You sat there and time passed you by, and it would never come back. There was immortality, for death had never been. Nothing existed except that immense tree, the clouds and the earth. You went to that tree and sat down with it, and every day for many days it was a benediction of which you were only aware when you wandered away. You could never come back to it asking for more; there was never the more, the more was in the valley far below. Because it was not a manmade shrine, there was unfathomable sacredness which would never again leave you, for it was not yours.

In the early morning when the sun had not yet touched the tops of the trees, the deer and the bear were there; we watched each other, wide-eyed and wondering; the earth was common to us and fear was absent. The blue jays and the red squirrels would come soon; the squirrel was tame and friendly. You had nuts in your pocket, and it took them out of your hand. When the squirrel had had enough, the two jays would hop down from the branches, and the scolding would stop. And the day began.

Sensuality in the world of pleasure has become very important. Taste dictates and soon the habit of pleasure takes hold. Though it may harm the whole organism, pleasure dominates. Pleasure of the senses, of cunning and subtle thought, of words and the images of mind and hand, is the culture of education, the pleasure of violence and the pleasure of sex. Man is moulded to the shape of pleasure, and all existence, religious or otherwise, is the pursuit of it. The wild exaggerations of pleasure are the outcome of moral and intellectual conformity. When the mind is not free and aware, sensuality becomes a factor of corruption, which is what is going on in the modern world—the pleasure of money and sex dominate. When we have become second-hand human beings, the expression of sensuality is our freedom. Then love is pleasure and desire.

Organised entertainment, religious or commercial, makes for social and personal immorality; you cease to be responsible. Responding wholly to any challenge is to be responsible, totally committed. This cannot be when the very essence of thought is fragmentary and the pursuit of pleasure, in all its obvious and subtle forms, is the principal movement of existence. Pleasure is not joy. Joy and pleasure are entirely different things; the one is uninvited and the other cultivated, nurtured. One comes when the *me* is not, and the other is time-binding; where the one is, the other is not. Pleasure, fear and violence run together; they are inseparable companions. Learning from observation is action; the doing is the seeing.

In the evening when darkness was approaching, the jays and the squirrels had gone to bed. The evening star was just visible, and the noises of the day and memory had come to an end. The giant sequoias were motionless. They will go on beyond time. Only man dies, and the sorrow of it.

October 21, 1973

It was a moonless night and the Southern Cross was clear
over the palm trees. The sun wouldn't be up for many
hours yet. In that quiet darkness, all the stars were very
close to the earth and they were sparklingly bright; they
were a penetrating blue and the river was giving birth to
them. The Southern Cross was by itself without any other
stars around it. There was no breeze and the earth seemed
to stand still, weary of man's activity. It was going to be
a lovely morning after the heavy rains, and there wasn't
a cloud on the horizon. Orion had already set and the
morning star was on the far horizon. In the grove, frogs
were croaking in the nearby pond; they would become
silent for a while and wake up and begin again. The smell
of jasmine was strong in the air, and in the distance there
was chanting. But at that hour there was a breathless
silence, and its tender beauty was on the land. Meditation is
the movement of that silence.

In the walled garden, the noise of the day began. A baby
was being washed; it was oiled with great care, every part
of it; special oil for the head and another for the body;
each had its own fragrance and both were slightly heated.
The small child loved it; it was softly cooing to itself and
its fat little body was bright with oil. Then it was washed,
not with soap but with a special scented powder. The child
never cried; there seemed to be so much love and care. It
was dried and tenderly wrapped in a clean white cloth, fed

and put to bed to fall asleep immediately. It would grow up to be educated, trained to work, accepting the traditions, the new or old beliefs, to have children, to bear sorrow and the laughter of pain.

The mother came one day and asked, 'What is love? Is it care, is it trust, is it responsibility, is it pleasure between man and woman? Is it the pain of attachment and loneliness?'

You are bringing up your child with such care, with tireless energy, giving your life and time. You feel, perhaps unknowingly, responsible. You love it. But the narrowing effect of education will begin, will make it conform with punishment and reward to fit into the social structure. Education is the accepted means for the conditioning of the mind. What are we educated for—for endless work and to die? You have given tender care and affection, and does your responsibility cease when education begins? Is it love that will send him to war, to be killed after all that care and generosity? Your responsibility never ceases, which doesn't mean interference. Freedom is total responsibility, not only for your children but for all children on the earth. Is love attachment and its pain? Attachment breeds pain, jealousy and hatred. Attachment grows out of one's own shallowness, insufficiency, loneliness. Attachment gives a sense of being and identification with something, gives a sense of reality, of being. When that is threatened there is fear, anger and envy. Is all this love? Is pain and sorrow love? Is sensory pleasure love? Most fairly intelligent human beings verbally know all this; it is not too complicated. But they do not let all this go; they turn these facts into ideas and then struggle with the abstract concepts. They prefer to live with abstractions rather than with reality, with *what is*.

In the denial of what love is not, love is. Don't be afraid of the word *negation*. Negate all that is not love, then *what is* is compassion. What you are matters enormously for you are the world and the world is you. This is compassion.

Slowly the dawn was coming; in the eastern horizon there was a faint light, it was spreading and the Southern Cross began to fade. The trees took on their shapes, the frogs became silent, the morning star was lost in the greater light and a new day began. The flight of crows and the voices of man had begun, but the blessings of that early morning were still there.

October 22, 1973

In a small boat on the quiet, slow current of the river, all
the horizon from north to south, east to west was visible;
there wasn't a tree or house that broke the horizon; there
was not a cloud floating by. The banks were flat, stretching
on both sides far into the land and they held the wide
river. There were other small fishing boats; the fishermen
huddled at one end with their nets out. These men were
immensely patient. The sky and the earth met, and there
was vast space. In this measureless space, the earth and all
things had their existence; even this small boat carried along
by the strong current. Around the bend of the river, the
horizons extended as far as the eye could see, measureless
and infinite. Space became inexhaustible.

There must be this space for beauty and compassion.
Everything must have space, the living and the dead, the
rock on the hill and the bird on the wing. When there is
no space, there is death. The fishermen were singing, and
the sound of their song came down the river. Sound needs
space. The sound of a word needs space; a word makes its
own space, rightly pronounced. The river and the faraway
tree can only survive when they have space; without space,
all things wither. The river disappeared into the horizon,
and the fishermen were going ashore. The deep darkness of
the night was coming. The earth was resting from a weary
day, and the stars were on the waters. The vast space was

narrowed down into a small house of many walls. Even the large, palatial houses have walls shutting out that immense space, making it their own.

A painting must have space within it, even though it is put in a frame. A statue can only exist in space. Music creates the space it needs. The sound of a word not only makes space: it needs it to be heard. Thought can imagine the extension between two points, the distance and the measure; the interval between two thoughts is the space that thought makes. The continuous extension of time, movement and the interval between two movements of thought need space. Consciousness is within the movement of time and thought. Thought and time are measurable between two points, between the centre and the periphery. Consciousness, wide or narrow, exists where there is a centre, the *me* and the *not me*.

All things need space. If rats are enclosed in a restricted space, they destroy each other. The small birds sitting on a telegraph wire of an evening, have the needed space between each other. Human beings living in crowded cities are becoming violent. Where there is no space, outwardly and inwardly, every form of mischief and degeneration is inevitable. The conditioning of the mind through so-called education, religion, tradition and culture, gives little space to the flowering of the mind and heart. The belief, the experience according to that belief, the opinion,

the concepts, the word, is the *me*, the ego, the centre
which creates the limited space within whose border is
consciousness. The *me* has its being and its activity within
the small space it has created for itself. All its problems
and sorrows, its hopes and despairs, are within its own
frontiers, and there is no space. The known occupies all its
consciousness. Consciousness is the known. Within this
frontier there is no solution to all the problems human
beings have put together. And yet they won't let go; they
cling to the known or invent the unknown, hoping it will
solve their problems. The space which the *me* has built for
itself is its sorrow and the pain of pleasure. The gods don't
give you space, for theirs is yours. This vast, measureless
space lies outside the measure of thought, and thought is
the known. Meditation is the emptying of consciousness of
its content, the known, the *me*.

Slowly the oars took the boat up the sleeping river, and
the light of a house gave it the direction. It had been a long
evening. The sunset was gold, green and orange, and it
made a golden path on the water.

October 24, 1973

Way down in the valley were the dull lights of a small
village. It was dark, and the path was stony and rough.
The waving lines of the hills against the starlit sky were
deeply embedded in darkness, and a coyote was howling
somewhere nearby. The path had lost its familiarity, and
a scented breeze was coming up the valley. To be alone in
that solitude was to hear the voice of intense silence and
its great beauty. An animal was making a noise among
the bushes, frightened of attracting attention. It was quite
dark by now, and the world of that valley became deep in
its silence. The night air had special smells, a blend of all
the bushes that grow on the dry hills, that strong smell of
bushes that know the hot sun. The rains had stopped many
months ago; it wouldn't rain again for a very long time, and
the path was dry and dusty.

The great silence with its vast space held the night, and
every movement of thought became still. The mind itself
was the immeasurable space, and in that deep quietness
there was not a thing that thought had built. To be
absolutely nothing is to be beyond measure. The path went
down a steep incline and a small stream was saying many
things, delighted with its own voice. It crossed the path
several times and the two were playing a game together.
The stars were very close and some were looking down
from the hilltops. Still the lights of the village were a long
way off and the stars were disappearing over the high hills.

Be alone, without word and thought, but only watching and listening. The great silence showed that without it, existence loses its profound meaning and beauty.

To be a light to oneself denies all experience. The one who is experiencing as the experiencer needs experience to exist and, however deep or superficial, the need for it becomes greater. Experience is knowledge, tradition, and the experiencer separates himself to discern between the enjoyable and the painful, the comforting and the disturbing. The believer experiences according to his belief, according to his conditioning. These experiences are from the known, for recognition is essential; without it there is no experience. Every experience leaves a mark unless there is an ending to it as it arises. Every response to challenge is an experience, but when the response is from the known, challenge loses its newness and vitality; then there is conflict, disturbance and neurotic activity. The very nature of challenge is to question, to disturb, to awaken, to understand. But when that challenge is translated into the past, the present is avoided.

The conviction of experience is the negation of inquiry. Intelligence is the freedom to inquire, to investigate the *me* and the *not me*, the outer and the inner. Belief, ideologies and authority prevent insight which comes only with freedom. The desire for experience of any kind must be superficial or sensory, comforting or pleasurable, for desire, however intense, is the forerunner of thought, and thought is the outer. Thought may put together the inner, but it is still the outer. Thought will never find the new for it is old, it is never free. Freedom lies beyond thought. All the activity of thought is not love.

To be a light to oneself is the light of all others. To be a light to oneself is for the mind to be free from challenge and response, for the mind then is totally awake, wholly attentive. This attention has no centre, the one who is attentive, and so no border. As long as there is a centre, the *me*, there must be challenge and response, adequate or inadequate, pleasurable or sorrowful. The centre can never be a light to itself; its light is the artificial light of thought, and it has many shadows. Compassion is not the shadow of thought, but it is light, neither yours nor another's.

The path gradually entered the valley, and the stream went by the village to join the sea. But the hills remained changeless, and the hoot of an owl was the reply to another. And there was space for silence.

October 25, 1973

From where one sat on a rock, in an orange orchard,
the valley spread out and disappeared into the fold of
mountains. It was early in the morning and the shadows
were long, soft and open. The quails were calling with
their sharp demand and the mourning dove was cooing,
with a soft, gentle lilt, a sad song so early in the morning.
The mockingbird was making swooping curves in the
air, turning somersaults, delighted with the world. A big
tarantula, hairy and dark, slowly came out from under the
rock, stopped, felt the morning air and unhurriedly went its
way. The orange trees were in long straight lines, acre upon
acre, with their bright fruit and fresh blossom—flower and
fruit on the same tree at the same time. The smell of these
blossoms was quietly pervasive, and with the heat of the sun
the smell would get deeper and more insistent. The sky was
very blue and soft, and all the hills and mountains were still
dreaming.

It was a lovely morning, cool and fresh, with that
strange beauty which man had not yet destroyed. The
lizards came out and sought a warm spot in the sun; they
stretched out to get their bellies warm, and their long tails
turned sideways. It was a happy morning, and the soft light
covered the land and the endless beauty of life. Meditation
is the essence of this beauty, expressed or silent. Expressed,
it takes form, substance; silent it is not to be put into

words, form or colour. From silence, expression, action is beauty and whole, and all struggle and conflict ceases. The lizards were moving into the shade and the hummingbirds and the bees were among the blossoms.

Without passion, there is no creation. Total abandonment brings this unending passion. Abandonment with a motive is one thing, and without a purpose, without calculation, it is another. That which has an end, a direction, is short-lived, becomes mischievous and commercial, vulgar. The other, not driven by any cause, intention or gain, has no beginning and no end. This abandonment is the emptying of the mind of the *me*, the self. This *me* can lose itself in activity, in some comforting belief or fanciful dream, but such loss is the continuing of the self in another form, identifying with another ideology and action. The abandonment of the self is not an act of will, for the will is the self. Any movement of the self, horizontally or vertically, in any direction, is still within the field of time and sorrow.

Thought may give itself over to something, sane or insane, reasonable or idiotic, but being in its very structure and nature fragmentary, its very enthusiasm and excitement, soon turn into pleasure and fear. In this area, the abandonment of the self is illusory, with little meaning. The awareness of all this is the awakening to the activities of the self; in this attention there is no centre, no self. The urge to express oneself for identification is the outcome of confusion and the meaninglessness of existence. To seek meaning is the beginning of fragmentation; thought can and does give a thousand meanings to life, each one inventing its own meanings which are merely opinions and convictions, and there is no end to them. The very living is the whole meaning, but when life is a conflict, a struggle, a battlefield of ambition, competition and the worship of success, the search for power and position, then life has no meaning.

What is the need of expression? Does creation lie in the thing produced? The thing produced by hand or by the mind, however beautiful or utilitarian—is that what one is after? Does this self-abandoned passion need expression? When there is a need, a compulsion, is it the passion of creation? As long as there is division between creator and the created, beauty and love come to an end. You may produce a most excellent thing in colour or in stone, but if your daily life contradicts that supreme excellence—the total abandonment of the self—that which you have produced is for admiration and vulgarity. The very living is the colour, the beauty and its expression. One needs no other.

The shadows were losing their distance, and the quails were quiet. There was only the rocks, the trees with their blossom and fruit, the lovely hills and the abundant earth.

October 29, 1973

In the valley of orange orchards, this one was very well looked after—row upon row of young trees, strong and sparkling in the sun. The soil was good, well-watered, manured and cared for. It was a beautiful morning with a clear blue sky, and the warm air was softly pleasant. The quails in the bushes were fussing about, with their sharp calls; a sparrowhawk was hovering in the air, motionless, and soon it came down to sit on a branch in the next orange tree and went to sleep. It was so close that the claws, the marvellous speckled feathers and the sharp beak were clearly visible; it was within the reach of an arm. Earlier in the morning, it had been along the avenue of mimosa, and the small birds cried out their alarm.

Under the bushes, two kingsnakes, with their dark brown rings along the length of their bodies, were curling around each other, and as they passed close by, they were utterly unaware of a human presence. They had been on a shelf in the shed, stretched out, their dark, bright eyes watching and waiting for mice. They stared without blinking for they had no eyelids. They must have been there during the night, and now they were among the bushes. It was their ground, and they were seen often. On picking one of them up, it coiled around the arm and felt cold to the touch. All those living things seemed to have their own order, their own discipline and their own play and gaiety.

Materialism, that nothing exists but matter, is the prevailing and persistent activity of human beings who are affluent and those who are not. Much of the world is dedicated to materialism; the structure of society is based on this formula, with all its consequences. Others are also materialistic, but idealistic principles are accepted when it is convenient and discarded under the name of rationality and necessity. In changing the environment, violently or slowly, revolution or evolution, the behaviour of man is changed according to the culture in which he lives. It is an age-old conflict between those who believe man is matter and those who pursue the spirit. This division has brought such misery, confusion and illusion to man.

Thought is material and all its activity, outer or inner, is materialistic. Thought is measurable, and so it is time. Within this area, consciousness is matter. Consciousness is its content; the content is consciousness; they are inseparable. The content is the many things thought has put together: the past modifying the present, which is the future, which is time. Time is movement within the area of consciousness, expanded or contracted. Thought is memory, experience and knowledge, and this memory, with its images and shadows, is the self, the *me* and the *not me*, *we* and *they*. The essence of division is the self with all its attributes and qualities.

Materialism only gives strength and growth to the self. The self identifies itself with the State, with an ideology, with activities of the *non-me*, religious or secular, but it is still the self. Its beliefs are self-created, as are its pleasures and fears. Thought by its very nature and structure is fragmentary, and conflict and war are between the various fragments, the nationalities, the races and ideologies. Materialistic humanity will destroy itself unless the self is wholly abandoned.

The abandonment of the self is always of primary importance. And only from this revolution can a new society be put together. The abandonment of the self is love, compassion: passion for all—the starving, the suffering, the homeless, and for the materialist and the believer. Love is not sentimentality or romanticism; it is as strong and final as death.

Slowly the fog from the sea came over the western hills like huge waves; it folded itself over the hills and down into the valley, and it would presently reach up here. It would become cooler with the coming darkness of the night. There would be no stars, and there would be complete silence. It is a factual silence and not the silence which thought has cultivated, in which there is no space.

MALIBU

April 1, 1975

Even so early in the morning, the sun was hot and burning.
There was no breeze and not a leaf was stirring. In the
ancient temple it was cool and pleasant; the bare feet were
aware of the solid slabs of rocks, their shapes and their
unevenness. Many thousands of people must have walked
on them for a thousand years. It was dark there after the
glare of the morning sun, and in the corridors there were
few people. In the narrow passage, it was darker still. This
passage led to a wide corridor which led to the inner shrine.
There was a strong smell of flowers and the incense of
many centuries.

A hundred Brahmins, freshly bathed, in newly washed
white loincloths, were chanting. Sanskrit is a powerful
language, resonant with depth. The ancient walls were
vibrating, almost shaking to the sound of a hundred voices.
The dignity of the sound was incredible, and the sacredness
of the moment was beyond the words. It was not the

words that awakened this immensity but the depth of the
sound, the sound of many thousand years held within these
walls and in the immeasurable space beyond them. It was
not the meaning of those words, nor the clarity of their
pronunciation, nor the dark beauty of the temple, but the
quality of sound that broke the walls and limitations of the
human mind. The song of a bird, a distant flute, a breeze
among the leaves—all these break down the walls that
human beings have created for themselves.

In the great cathedrals and lovely mosques, the chants
and the intoning of their sacred books, it is the sound
that opens the heart, to tears and beauty. Without space,
there is no beauty; without space, you have only walls and
measurement; without space, there is no depth; without
space, there is poverty, inner and outer. You have so little
space in your mind; it is so crammed full of words and
remembrances, knowledge, experiences and problems.
There is hardly any space left, only the endless chatter of
thought. And so your museums are filled and every shelf
with books. Then you fill the places of entertainment,
religious or otherwise. Or you build a wall around yourself,
a narrow space of mischief and pain. Without space, inner
and outer, you become violent and ugly.

Everything needs space to live, to play and to chant.
That which is sacred cannot live without space. You have
no space when you hold, when there is sorrow, when you
become the centre of the universe. The space that you

occupy is the space that thought has built around you, and that is misery and confusion. The space that thought measures is the division between you and me, we and they. This division is endless pain.

There is that solitary tree in the wide, green, open field.

April 2, 1975

It was not a land of trees, meadows, streams, flowers
and mirth. It was a sunburnt land of sand and barren
hills, without a single tree or bush; a land of desolation,
endless scorched earth, mile upon mile. There wasn't a
bird and not even oil; there were no derricks or flames.
Consciousness could not hold the desolation, and every hill
was a barren shadow. For many hours we flew over this vast
emptiness, and at last there were snow peaks, forests and
streams, villages and towns.

You may have a great deal of knowledge and be vastly
poor. The poorer you are, the greater the demand for
knowledge. You expand your consciousness with great
varieties of knowledge, accumulating experiences and
remembrances and yet are vastly poor. The skilful use of
knowledge may bring you wealth and give you eminence
and power, but there may still be poverty. This poverty
breeds callousness; you play while the house is burning.
This poverty merely strengthens the intellect or gives to
the emotions the weakness of sentiment. It is this poverty
that brings about imbalance, lack of harmony, conflict
of division between the outer and inner. There is no
knowledge of the inner, only of the outer. The knowledge
of the outer informs us erroneously that there must be
knowledge of the inner. Self-knowing is brief and shallow;
the mind is soon beyond it, like crossing a river. You
make a lot of noise going across the river, and to mistake

the noise as knowledge of the self is to expand poverty.
This expansion of consciousness is the activity of poverty.
Religion, culture and knowledge can in no way enrich
this poverty.

The skill of intelligence is to put knowledge in its right
place. Without knowledge, it is not possible to live in
this technological and almost mechanical civilisation, but
it will not transform the human being and his society.
Knowledge is not the excellence of intelligence; intelligence
can and does use knowledge and thus transforms man
and his society. Intelligence is not the mere cultivation
of the intellect and its integrity. It comes out of the
understanding of the whole consciousness of man, yourself,
not a part, a separate segment, of yourself. The study and
the understanding of the movement of your own mind and
heart give birth to this intelligence. You are the content of
your consciousness; in knowing yourself, you will know the
universe. This knowing is beyond the word, for the word is
not the thing. The freedom from the known, every minute,
is the essence of intelligence. It is this intelligence that is
in operation in the universe if you leave it alone. You are
destroying this sacredness of order through the ignorance
of yourself. This ignorance is not banished by the studies
others have made about you or themselves. You yourself
have to study the content of your own consciousness.
The studies others have made of themselves, and so of
yourself, are the descriptions but not the described. The
word is not the thing.

Only in relationship can you know yourself, not in abstraction and certainly not in isolation. Even in a monastery, you are related to the society which has made the monastery as an escape, or closed the doors to freedom. The movement of behaviour is the sure guide to yourself; it is the mirror of your consciousness. This mirror will reveal its content, the images, the attachments, the fears, the loneliness, the joy and the sorrow. Poverty lies in the running away from this, either in its sublimations or in its identities. Negating without resistance this content of consciousness is the beauty and compassion of intelligence.

April 3, 1975

How extraordinarily beautiful is the great curve of a wide
river. You must see it from a certain height, not too far up
or too close as it meanders lazily through the green fields.
The river was wide, full of water, blue and clear. We were
not flying at a great altitude and we could just see the
strong current in the middle of the river with its tiny waves;
we followed it past towns and villages to the sea. Each curve
had its own beauty, its own strength, its own movement.
And far away were the great snow-covered peaks, pink in
the early morning light; they covered the eastern horizon.
The wide river and those great mountains seemed to
hold, for that hour, eternity—this overwhelming sense of
timeless space. Though the plane was rushing southeast, in
that space there was no direction, no movement, only that
which is. For a whole hour, there was nothing else, not even
the noise of the jets. Only when the captain announced
that we would soon be landing did that full hour come to
an end. There was no memory of that hour, no record of its
content, and so thought had no hold on it. When it came
to an end, there were no remains; the slate was clean again.
Thought had no means to cultivate that hour and so it got
ready to leave the plane.

What thought thinks about is made into a reality, but it
is not truth. Beauty can never be the expression of thought.
A bird is not made by thought, and so it is beautiful.

Love is not shaped by thought, and when it is, it becomes something quite different. The worship of the intellect and its integrity is a reality made by thought. But it is not compassion. Thought cannot manufacture compassion; it makes it into a reality, a necessity, and so it can never be compassion. Thought by its very nature is fragmentary and so it lives in a fragmented world of division and conflict. So knowledge is fragmentary, and however much it is piled up, layer after layer, it will remain fragmented, broken up. Thought can put together a thing called integration, and that too will be a fragment.

The very word *science* means knowledge, and through knowledge we hope we will be transformed into a sane and happy human being. And so man is eagerly pursuing knowledge of all the things of the earth and of himself. Knowledge is not compassion, and without compassion knowledge breeds mischief and untold misery and chaos. Knowledge cannot make man love another; it can create war and the instruments of destruction but cannot bring love to the heart or peace to the mind. To perceive all this is to act, but not an action based on memory and patterns. Love is not memory, a remembrance of pleasures.

April 4, 1975

By chance it happened that one lived alone for some
months in a small dilapidated house, high in the
mountains, far from other houses. There were lots of trees,
and as it was spring there was perfume in the air. The
solitude was of the mountains and of the beauty of the
red earth. The towering peaks were covered with snow,
and some of the trees were in bloom. One lived alone
amidst this splendour. The forest was nearby, with deer,
an occasional bear and those big monkeys with black faces
and long tails. Of course, there were serpents too. In deep
solitude, in strange ways, one was related to them all. One
could not hurt a thing, even that white daisy on the path.
In that relationship, the space between you and them did
not exist; it was not contrived; it was not an intellectual
or an emotional conviction that brought this about, but
simply it was so.

A group of those large monkeys would come around,
especially in the evenings; a few on the ground but most
of them sitting in the trees quietly watching. Surprisingly
they were still; occasionally there would be a scratch or
two, and we would watch each other. They would come
every evening now, neither too close nor too high among
the trees, and we would be silently aware of each other. We
had become quite good friends, but they didn't want to
encroach upon one's solitude. Walking one afternoon in

the forest, one came suddenly upon them in an open space. There must have been well over thirty of them, young and old, sitting among the trees around the open space, absolutely silent and still. One could have touched them; there was no fear in them, and sitting on the ground we watched each other until the sun went behind the peaks.

If you lose touch with nature, you lose touch with humanity. If there is no relationship with nature you become a killer; then you kill baby seals, whales, dolphins and man, either for gain, for sport, for food or for knowledge. Then nature is frightened of you, withdrawing its beauty. You may take long walks in the woods or camp in lovely places, but you are a killer and so lose their friendship. You are probably not related to anything, to your wife or husband; you are much too busy gaining and losing, with your own private thoughts, pleasures and pains. You live in your own dark isolation, and the escape from it is further darkness. Your interest is in a short survival, mindless, easygoing or violent. And thousands die of hunger or are butchered because of your irresponsibility. You leave the ordering of the world to the lying corrupt politician, to the intellectuals, to the experts. Because you have no integrity, you build a society that is immoral, dishonest, a society based on utter selfishness. And then you escape from all this, for which you alone are responsible, to the beaches, the woods, or carry a gun for 'sport'.

You may know all this, but knowledge does not bring about transformation in you. You have to act integrally as a total human being. Then when you have this sense of the whole, you will be related to the universe.

April 6, 1975

It is not that extraordinary blue of the Mediterranean; the Pacific has an ethereal blue, especially when there is a gentle breeze from the west. As you drive north along the coast road, the sea is so tender, dazzling, clear and full of mirth. Occasionally you would see whales blowing on their way north and rarely their enormous heads as they threw themselves out of the water. There was a whole pod of them, blowing. They must be very powerful animals. That day the sea was a lake, still and utterly quiet, without a single wave; there was not that clear dancing blue. The sea was asleep, and you watched it with wonder.

The house overlooks the sea. It is a beautiful house, with a quiet garden, a green lawn and flowers. It is a spacious house, with the light of the Californian sun. And rabbits loved it too; they would come early in the morning and late in the evening; they would eat up flowers and the newly planted pansies, marigolds and small flowering plants. You couldn't keep them out though there was wire netting all around, and to kill them would be a crime. But a cat and a barn owl brought order; the black cat wandered about the garden; the owl perched itself during the day among the thick eucalyptus. You could see it, motionless, eyes closed, round and big. The rabbits disappeared and the garden flourished. The blue Pacific flowed effortlessly.

It is only man that brings disorder to the universe.
He is ruthless and extremely violent. Wherever he is, he
brings misery and confusion in himself and in the world
about him. He lays waste and destroys, and he has no
compassion. In himself there is no order and so what he
touches becomes soiled and chaotic. His politics have
become refined gangsterism of power, deceit, personal or
national, group against group. His economy is restricted
and so not universal. His society is immoral, in freedom
and under tyranny. He is not religious though he believes,
worships and goes through endless, meaningless rituals.
Why has he become like this—cruel, irresponsible and so
utterly self-centred? Why?

There are a hundred explanations, and those who
explain, subtly with words born of the knowledge of many
books, are caught in the net of human sorrow, ambition,
pride and agony. The description is not the described;
the word is not the thing. Is it because he is looking for
outward causes, the environment conditioning man,
hoping the outer change transforms the inner man? Is it
because he is so attached to his senses, dominated by their
immediate demands? Is it because he lives so entirely in
the movement of thought and knowledge? Is it because he
is so romantic, sentimental, that he becomes ruthless with
his ideals, make-believe and pretensions? Is it because he is
always led, a follower, or becomes a leader or guru?

This division as the outer and inner is the beginning of his conflict and misery; he is caught in contradiction, in ageless tradition. Caught in this meaningless division, he is lost and becomes a slave to others. The outer and inner are the imagination and invention of thought. As thought is fragmentary, it makes for disorder and conflict, which is division. Thought cannot bring about order, an effortless flow of virtue. Virtue is not the continuous repetition of memory or practice.

Thought-knowledge is time-binding. Thought by its very nature and structure cannot grasp the whole flow of life as a total movement. Thought-knowledge cannot have an insight into this wholeness; it cannot be aware of this choicelessly as long as it remains as the perceiver, the outsider looking in. Thought-knowledge has no place in perception. The thinker is the thought; the perceiver is the perceived. Only then is there an effortless movement in our daily life.

OJAI

April 8, 1975

In this part of the world, it doesn't rain much, about fifteen to twenty inches a year, and these rains are most welcome for it doesn't rain for the rest of the year. There is snow then on the mountains, but during summer and autumn they are bare, sunburnt, rocky and forbidding; only in the spring are they mellow and welcoming. There used to be bear, deer, bobcat, quail and any number of rattlers. But now they are disappearing; the dreaded man is encroaching. It had rained for some time now, and the valley was green. The orange trees bore fruit and flower. It is a beautiful valley, quiet away from the town, and you heard the mourning dove. The air was slowly being filled with the scent of orange blossoms, and in a few days it would be overpowering, with the warm sun and windless days.

It was a valley wholly surrounded by hills and mountains; beyond the hills was the sea and beyond the mountains desert. In the summer it would be unbearably hot, but there was always beauty here, far from the maddening crowd and their cities. And at night there would be extraordinary silence, rich and penetrating. Cultivated meditation is a sacrilege to beauty, and every leaf and branch spoke of the joy of beauty. The tall, dark cypress was silent with it; the gnarled old pepper tree flowed with it.

You cannot, may not, invite joy; if you do, it becomes pleasure. Pleasure is the movement of thought and thought may not, can in no way, cultivate joy. If it pursues that which has been joyous, then it is only a remembrance, a dead thing. Beauty is never timebinding; it is wholly free of time and so of culture. It is there when the self is not. The self is put together by time, by the movement of thought, by the known, by the word. In the abandonment of the self, in that total attention, that essence of beauty is there. The letting go of the self is not the calculated action of desire-will. Will is directive, resistant, divisive, and so breeds conflict. The dissolution of the self is not the evolution of knowledge of the self; time does not enter into it at all. There is no way or means to end it. The total inward nonaction is the positive attention of beauty.

You have cultivated a vast network of interrelated activities in which you are caught, and your mind, being conditioned by it, operates inwardly in the same manner. Achievement then becomes the most important thing, and the fury of that drive is still the skeleton of the self. That is why you follow your guru, your saviour, your beliefs and ideals; faith takes the place of insight and awareness. There is no need for prayer or rituals when the self is not. You fill the empty spaces of the skeleton with knowledge, images and meaningless activities, and so keep it seemingly alive.

In the quiet stillness of the mind, that which is everlasting beauty comes, uninvited, unsought, without the noise of recognition.

April 10, 1975

In the silence of the deep night and in the quiet, still morning when the sun is touching the hills, there is a great mystery. It is there in all living things. If you sat quietly under a tree, you would feel the ancient earth with its incomprehensible mystery. On a still night when the stars are clear and close, you would be aware of expanding space and the mysterious order of all things, of the immeasurable and of nothing, of the movement of the dark hills and the hoot of an owl. In that utter silence of the mind, this mystery expands without time and space. There is mystery in those ancient temples built with infinite care, with attention which is love. The slender mosques and the great cathedrals lose this shadowy mystery, for there is bigotry, dogma and military pomp.

The myth that is concealed in the deep layers of the mind is not mysterious; it is romantic, traditional and conditioned. In the secret recesses of the mind, truth has been pushed aside by symbols, words and images. In them there is no mystery; they are the churnings of thought. In knowledge and its action, there is wonder, appreciation and delight. But mystery is quite another thing. It is not an experience, to be recognised, stored up and remembered. Experience is the death of that incommunicable mystery; to communicate you need words, gestures, a look, but to be in communion with that, the mind, the whole of you must be at the same level, at the same time, with the same intensity as that which is called mysterious. This is love. With this, the whole mystery of the universe is open.

This morning there wasn't a cloud in the sky, the sun was in the valley, and all things were rejoicing, except man. He looked at this wondrous earth and went on with his labour, his sorrow and passing pleasures. He had no time to see; he was too occupied with his problems, agonies and violence. He does not see the tree, and so he cannot see his own travail. When he is forced to look, he tears to pieces what he sees, which he calls analysis, runs away from it or doesn't want to see. In the art of seeing lies the miracle of transformation, the transformation of *what is*. *What should be* never is. There is vast mystery in the act of seeing. This needs care and attention, which is love.

April 14, 1975

A large serpent was crossing a wide road just ahead of you,
fat, heavy, moving lazily. It was coming from a pond a little
way off. It was almost black and the light of the evening
sun falling on it gave to its skin a high polish. It moved in a
leisurely way with lordly dignity of power. It was unaware
of you as you stood quietly watching; you were quite close
to it. It must have measured well over five feet, and it was
bulging with what it had eaten. It went over a mound, and
you walked towards it, looking down upon it a few inches
away, its forked black tongue darting in and out. It was
moving towards a large hole. You could have touched it for
it had a strange attractive beauty. A villager was passing by
and called out to leave it alone because it was a cobra.

The next day the villagers had put there on the mound
a saucer of milk and some hibiscus flowers. On that same
road, further along, there was a bush, high and almost
leafless, that had thorns almost two inches long, sharp,
greyish, and no animal would dare to touch its succulent
leaves. It was protecting itself and woe to anyone that
touched it. There were deer in those woods, shy and very
curious; they would allow themselves to be approached
but not too close, and if you did they would dart away
and disappear among the undergrowth. There was one,
bright-eyed with its large ears forward, that would let you
come quite close if you were alone. They all had white spots

on a russet-brown skin; they were gentle and everwatchful, and it was pleasant to be among them. There was a completely white one, which must have been a freak.

The good is not the opposite of evil. It has never been touched by that which is evil, though it is surrounded by it. Evil cannot hurt the good, but the good may appear to do harm, and so evil gets more cunning, more mischievous. Evil can be cultivated and sharpened. It is expansively violent. It is born within the movement of time, nurtured and skilfully used. But goodness is not of time; it can in no way be cultivated or nurtured by thought. Its action is not visible; it has no cause and so no effect. Evil cannot become good, for that which is good is not the product of thought; it lies beyond thought, like beauty. The thing that thought produces, thought can undo, but it is not the good. As it is not of time, the good has no abiding place. Where the good is, there is order, but not the order of authority, punishment and reward. This order is essential, for otherwise society destroys itself, and man becomes evil, murderous, corrupt and degenerate. For man is society; they are inseparable. The law of the good is everlasting, unchanging and timeless. Stability is its nature, and so it is utterly secure. There is no other security.

April 17, 1975

Space is order. Space is time, length, width and volume. This morning the sea and the heavens are immense; the horizon where those yellow-flowered hills meet the distant sea is the order of earth and heaven; it is cosmic. That cypress, tall, dark, alone, has the order of beauty, and the distant house on that wooded hill follows the movement of the mountains that tower over the low-lying hills. The green field with a single cow is beyond time. And the man coming up the hill is held within the narrow space of his problems.

There is a space of nothingness whose volume is not bound by time and the measure of thought. This space the mind cannot enter; it can only observe. In this observation, there is no experiencer. This observer has no history, no association, no myth, and so the observer is that which is. Knowledge is extensive but it has no space, for by its very weight and volume it perverts and smothers that space. There is no knowledge of the self, higher or lower; there is only a verbal structure of the self, a skeleton, covered over by thought. Thought cannot penetrate its own structure; what it has put together thought cannot deny, and when it does deny, it is the refusal of further gain. When the time of the self is not, the space that has no measure is.

This measure is the movement of reward and punishment, gain or loss, the activity of comparison and conformity, of respectability and the very denial of it. This movement is time, the future with its hope, and attachment which is the past. This complex network is the very structure of the self, and its union with the supreme being or the ultimate principle is still within its own field. All this is the activity of thought. Thought can in no way penetrate that space of no time, do what it will. The very method, the curriculum, the practice that thought has invented are not the keys that will open the door, for there is no door, no key. Thought can only be aware of its own endless activity, its own capacity to corrupt, its own deceits and illusions. It is the observer and the observed. Its gods are its own projections, and the worship of them is the worship of yourself. What lies beyond thought, beyond the known, may not be imagined or made a myth of or made a secret for the few. It is there for you to see.

MALIBU

April 23, 1975

The wide river was still as a millpond. There wasn't a ripple
and the morning breeze hadn't awakened yet, for it was
early. The stars were in the water, clear and sparkling, and
the morning star was the brightest. The trees across the
river were dark, and the village amongst them still slept.
There was not a leaf stirring, and those small screech owls
were rattling away on the old tamarind tree; it was their
home, and when the sun was on those branches they
would be warming themselves. The noisy green parrots
were quiet too. All things, even the insects and the cicadas,
were waiting, breathless for the sun, in adoration. The river
was motionless, and the usual small boats with their lamps
were absent.

Gradually over the dark, mysterious trees there began
the early light of dawn. Every living thing was still in the
mystery of that moment; it was the timeless moment of
meditation. Your own mind was timeless, without measure;

there was no yardstick to measure how long that moment lasted. Only there was a stirring and an awakening—the parrots and the owls, the crows and the mynah, the dogs and a voice across the river. And suddenly the sun shone through the trees, golden and hidden by the leaves. Now the great river was awake, moving; time, length, width and volume were flowing, and all life began which never ended.

How lovely it was that morning, the purity of light and the golden path the sun made on those living waters. You were the world, the cosmos, the deathless beauty and the joy of compassion. Only you were not there; if you were all this would not be. You bring in the beginning and the ending, to begin again in an endless chain.

In becoming, there is uncertainty and instability. In nothingness, there is absolute stability and so clarity. That which is wholly stable never dies; corruption is in becoming. The world is bent on becoming, achieving, gaining, and so there is the fear of losing and dying. The mind must go through that small hole which it has put together, the self, to come upon this vast nothingness whose stability thought cannot measure. Thought desires to capture it, use it, cultivate it and put it on the market. It must be made acceptable and respectable, to be worshipped. Thought cannot put it into any category, and so it must be a delusion and a snare; or it must be for the few, for the select. And so thought goes about its mischievous ways, frightened, cruel, vain and never stable, though its conceit asserts there is stability in its actions, in its exploration, in the knowledge it has accumulated. The dream becomes a reality which it has nurtured. What thought has made real is not truth. Nothingness is not a reality, but it is the truth. The small hole, the self, is the reality of thought, the skeleton on which it has built all its existence—the reality of its fragmentation, pain, sorrow and its love. The reality of its gods, or its one God, is the careful structure of thought, its prayer, its rituals, its romantic worship. In reality, there is no stability or pure clarity.

The knowledge of the self is time, length, width and volume; it can be accumulated, used as a ladder to become, to improve, to achieve. This knowledge will in no way free the mind of the burden of its own reality. You are the burden; the truth of it lies in the seeing of it, and that freedom is not the reality of thought. The seeing is the doing. The doing comes from the stability and clarity of nothingness.

April 24, 1975

Every living thing has its own sensitivity, its own way of
life, its own consciousness, but man assumes that his own
is far superior and thereby he loses his love, his dignity, and
becomes insensitive, callous and destructive.

In the valley of orange trees, with their fruit and spring
blossom, it was a lovely clear morning. The mountains to
the north had a sprinkling of snow on them; they were
bare, hard and aloof, but against the tender blue sky of
early morning they were very close; you could almost
touch them. They had that immense sense of age and
indestructible majesty and the beauty that comes with
timeless grandeur.

It was a very still morning, and the smell of orange
blossom filled the air. There was the wonder and beauty
of light. The light of this part of the world has a special
quality, penetrating, alive and filling the eyes; it seemed to
enter into your whole consciousness, sweeping away any
dark corners. There was great joy in that, and every leaf and
blade of grass was rejoicing in it. The blue jay was hopping
from branch to branch and not screeching its head off for a
change. It was a lovely morning of light and great depth.

Time has bred consciousness with its content. It is
the culture of time. Its content makes up consciousness;
without it, consciousness, as we know it, is not. Then there

is nothing. We move the little pieces in consciousness from one area to another, according to the pressure of reason and circumstance but in the same field of pain, sorrow and knowledge. This movement is time, the thought and the measure. It is a senseless game that most play, the worthy and the foolish; it is a game of hide and seek with yourself, the shadow and substance of thought, the past and the future of thought. Thought cannot hold this moment, for this moment is not of time. This moment is the ending of time; time has stopped at that moment; there is no movement at that moment, and so it is not related to another moment. It has no cause and so no beginning and no end. Consciousness cannot contain it. In that moment of nothingness, everything is. Meditation is the emptying of consciousness of its content.

[The additional pages of the Journal begin here.
The places where they were written were not noted by
Krishnamurti and have been added at publication.]

GSTAAD

August 3, 1981

The valley runs from east to west; the east end tapers off
to a narrow canyon with a six-thousand-foot mountain,
over which the morning sun comes, casting long, deep
shadows and endless silences. There is an oak tree, several
hundred years old, which catches the morning sun, golden
and motionless. The very highest leaf, there are only three
of them, is breathless in breathless stillness. The mourning
dove begins its peculiar, long, soft cooing, replied to by its
mate. And the day has begun. The barn owl had stopped
its hooting as the early spring morning was showing the
outlines of the nearby mountain and the long lines of
wooded hills. Before the sun actually comes up, great
silence seems to cover the land. And how beautiful the
earth is, timeless in its vastness. It is our earth, ours and not
of any group, community or nation. It is ours; it belongs to
every one of us.

The road is well-engineered, smooth, wide, without too many sharp turns as it climbs, passing mile upon mile of well-kept orange orchards and endless avocado groves which go down the gullies and up the whole hillside, curving over the top; all to be watered and cared for. The valley is filled with the scent of orange blossom and the avocado. The road passes through the enchanted land, ever climbing, until it reaches perhaps five thousand feet. Then it descends slowly into the desert.

At the highest point of the road, we stopped the car. To the south, the high hills were covered with trees and bushes, purple and yellow flowers; to the north there were no trees; it was barren, rocky, vast, stretching to the horizon, utterly unspoiled. Every tree, bush and rock was as it must have been for a thousand years. The immense space and measureless silence! Solitude is one thing, and being alone is another. Solitude can be isolation, an escape, an unwanted thing, but to be alone without the burden of life, with that utter freedom in which time-thought has never been, is to be with the universe.

In solitude is despairing loneliness, a sense of being abandoned, lost, craving for some kind of relationship, like a ship lost at sea. Our daily activity leads to this isolation, with its endless conflicts and miseries and rare joys thrown in. This solitude is corruption, manifested in politics, in business and of course in organised religions. Corruption exists in the very high places and on the very doorstep.

To be tied is corruption; any form of attachment leads to it, whether it be to a belief, faith, ideal, experience or any conclusion. Psychological corruption is a common factor in the human being. Money, status and power are the superficial responses of this inward corruption of mounting pleasure, desire, and the image that thought builds around the movement of desire. Corruption is fragmentation.

In that vast space between the blue, clear sky and the beauty of the earth, consciousness had come to an end. All the senses were fully awake to the unpolluted air, the smell of the desert and distant flowers, the movement of the lizard on the warm rock and the utter silence. It was not only the silence of high altitude, or of that strange silence just after the sun has set, or of that which seemed to descend on the earth with the beginning of dawn, away from the noisy cities and towns, but also that profound silence which the noise of thought has never touched. It is that silence that has no measure, of such purity and clarity that goes far beyond the movement of consciousness. Time had literally stopped.

But that silence accompanied as the car ran down through the orchards and the groves. Then civilisation began, the incredible vulgarity, the brutal haste and the immodesty of humans, everyone asserting their presence, and the rich showing off their power and will. Even that excellent motor seemed to have become suddenly silent, which of course is nonsense. The morning papers in their editorials were stating what the effect would be if and when a nuclear bomb exploded over a great city: several million vaporised, society in ruins and primordial chaos. And so on, horror upon horror. And humanity puts its faith in politicians and governments.

Any specialisation—the surgeon, the archbishop, the clerk or the plumber—uses only a part of the brain, narrowing down its total activity. The politician and the guru employ only a small part of the extraordinary capacity and energy of the brain. This limited, partial activity is creating havoc in the world. This small part of the brain is functioning in religions when they repeat their rituals, their meaningless words, their gestures of two or five thousand years of tradition, according to what has been programmed. Some do it gracefully in fine garments, and others crudely. It is the same in government circles with the corruption of power. The little part may accumulate great knowledge, but that very knowledge and research only further strengthen the small part of the brain.

The ascension of man can never be through knowledge, for it is never complete; it is ever within the shadow of ignorance. The ultra-intelligent machine, the fast-developing computer, programmed by experts, will overtake and outrun man's thought and its slow capacities; it will learn faster, correcting its own mistakes, solving its own problems.

The human being has not resolved any of his psychological problems, the issues that have become so complex. It appears that he has been burdened with them from the most ancient of days. We are still carrying on with these problems, of government, religion, relationship, violence, wars and the pollution of the earth. They will remain insoluble as long as only a part of the brain is functioning, as long as one is programmed to be American, British, French and so on. As long as one is a Catholic, Hindu, Muslim and so on, it appears one is so utterly unaware how conditioned, programmed that little part of the brain is. This programming gives an illusory sense of security, a verbal structure against the barbarians. But man is the only barbarian; he himself is the cause of all the corruption and terror that is taking place in the world. He is totally and completely responsible for all that is happening around him.

This little part of the brain is our consciousness; it is the seat of time, measure, space and thought. Time is evolution both biologically and psychologically. It is the sun rising and setting; it is chronological and psychological. Measure is *what is* and *what should be*, the ideal to be achieved, the violent becoming non-violent, the constant, continuous becoming; comparison, imitation, conformity, the better and the more. Space: there is the vast expanse of the earth, the heavens, and the little space in crowded cities; and space, if any, in consciousness.

Thought is the master. Thought is the most dominant factor in human life. There is no Eastern or Western thought; there is only thought, which may be experienced in many different ways, but is still the movement of thought. Thought is common to all mankind, from the most primitive to the most highly educated. Thought has put man on the moon; thought has built the atom bomb; it has built all the temples, the great cathedrals with all the things in them called sacred, the elaborate rituals, the dogmas, the beliefs, faith and so on. It has built the computer and the program that goes into it. It has helped mankind in different ways, but it has also bred wars and all the instruments of death. It has projected ideals, enormous violence, tortures, divided humanity into nations, classes, and invented religions which have divided man against himself. It has set man against man. Love is not thought with its remembrances and images. Thought sustains and nourishes consciousness. The content of consciousness is the never-ending movement of thought: the desires, conflicts, fears, the pursuit of pleasure, the pain, loneliness and sorrow.

Love and compassion, with its incorruptible intelligence, is beyond this limited consciousness. It may not be divided into higher or lower, for however high or low is still consciousness, ever noisy, ever chattering. It is all time and all measure, for it is born of thought. Thought can never be, under any circumstances, whole; it may speculate about

148

that which is whole and indulge in the verbalisation and the experience of it, but thought can never perceive its beauty, its intensity. For thought is the barren child of experience and knowledge which can never be complete, whole. So thought will always be limited, fragmented. The problems thought has brought to man, thought tries vainly to resolve, and this increasingly perpetuates them. Only when it realises its own incapacity, psychologically, to resolve the problems and conflicts it has brought about, only then perception and insight can end them.

August 7, 1981

The love of trees is, or should be, part of our nature, like breathing. They are part of the earth, like us, full of beauty, with a strange aloofness. They are so still, full of leaves, rich and full of light, casting long shadows, and wild with joy when there is a storm. Every leaf dances in the slight breeze, and the shadows are welcoming in the strong sun. As you sit with your back against the trunk, if you are very quiet, you establish a lasting relationship with nature. Most people have lost that relationship; they look at the mountains and valleys, the streams and the thousand trees, as they pass by in their cars or walking up the hill, chattering. They are too absorbed in their own problems to look and be quiet. The smoke is going up in a single column across the valley, and a lorry goes by down in the valley, heavy with logs of recently cut trees, their bark still on them. A group of boys and girls pass you by, chattering and shattering the still of the wood.

The death of a tree is beautiful in its ending, unlike man. A dead tree in a desert, stripped of its bark, polished by the sun and the winds, all its naked branches opened to the heavens, is a wondrous sight. A great redwood, many hundreds of years old, is cut down in a few minutes to make fences and seats, to build houses and to enrich the soil in a garden. That marvellous giant is gone. Man is pushing deeper and deeper into the forests, destroying them for pastures and houses. The wilds are disappearing. There is a valley whose surrounding hills are perhaps the oldest on earth, where the cheetahs, bears and deer one saw have entirely disappeared; for man is everywhere. The beauty of the earth is slowly being destroyed and polluted. Cars and tall buildings are appearing in the most unexpected of places. When you lose your relationship with nature and the vast heavens, you lose your relationship with man.

He came with his wife, and talked more than she; she was shy, intelligent looking. He was rather overbearing and appeared to be aggressive. She said they had been to some of the talks after reading one or two books, and heard some of the dialogues.

'We have come to talk over our major problems personally with you, which I hope you won't mind. We have two children, a boy and a girl; they are at school, fortunately for them. We don't want to inflict on them our ugly quarrels and conflicts. They will, though, hear of them soon enough. We two are very fond of each other; I won't use the word *love* as I have understood what you mean by that word. We married fairly young. We have a nice house with a garden; money is not our problem. We haven't come to you as a marriage counsellor, but we want to discuss our relationship with you if you don't mind. My wife is rather reserved, but I am sure she will join in the discussion presently. We had agreed that I would lead off. We are greatly troubled about our relationship. We have talked about it quite often, but nothing has come out of it. After this introduction, the question I would like to ask is, what is wrong with our relationship, or what is right relationship?'

What is your relationship with those clouds, full of evening light or with those silent trees? It is not an irrelevant question. Do you see those children playing in that field, and that old car? When you see these, what is your reaction, if one may ask?

'I am not sure. I like children shouting. So does my wife. I have no special feelings about those clouds and that tree. I have not thought about them; I have never really looked at them.'

The wife said, 'I have; they mean something to me that cannot be put into words. The children out there may be my children. After all, I am a mother.'

Do look, sir, at those clouds and the trees, as though you were looking for the first time. Look at them without thought interfering or wandering off. Look at them without naming them as a cloud or a tree. Just look with your heart and eyes. They are of the earth as we are, as those children are, even that old car. The very naming is part of thought.

'To look at those without verbalising seems almost impossible. The very form is the word.'

So words play a very important part in our lives; our life, it appears, is a complicated network of interrelated words. Words have a great impact on us, like *God, democracy, freedom, totalitarianism*. These words conjure up familiar images. The words *wife* and husband are part of our everyday currency. But the word *wife* is not actually the living person, with all her complexities. So the word is never the actual. When the word becomes all-important in living, the actual is neglected.

'But I can't escape from the word and the image the word brings up.'

One cannot separate the word and the image. The word is the image. To observe without word-images is the problem.

'That is impossible, sir.'

If one may point out again, you haven't attempted seriously to do this—the word *impossible* blocks your doing it. Don't, please, say it is possible or impossible, but simply do it. Let us go back to your question of what is right relationship. You will, one is sure, find out for yourself what is right when we understand relationship. What does relationship mean to you?

'Let me think. It means so many things depending on circumstances. One day it is a particular response and another it has a wholly different significance. It is responsibility, boredom, irritation, sensual responses and the urge to escape from it all.'

This is what you call relationship. It is different degrees of sensory responses, of sentiment and romanticism, if one is inclined that way, tenderness, attachment, loneliness, fear and so on—apprehensiveness more than actual fear. This is called relationship with a particular person or with others. You are also related to your ideals and hopes, to your experiences and conclusions. Your relationship is all this and more. All this is you and your relationship with another, and the other person is similar to you, though biologically, culturally and outwardly different. So does it not indicate that you are ever active within egocentrism and she is acting in a similar manner? Two parallel lines never meeting.

'I am beginning to see what you mean. Do please continue.'

It becomes clear that there is no actual relationship; each one is basically concerned about oneself, one's own pleasure, yielding to another in satisfaction and so on.

Let us put it differently. Why are human beings so self-centred, so consciously or in the deep recesses of their beings selfish? Why? The non-domesticated animals appear not to be so egocentric as humans. If we are to discover for ourselves what is right relationship, we must go into this question very deeply.

Perception without motive is to experiment. Most of us find it difficult to observe without some kind of motive or other, as we said before. Can we together examine, very objectively, what actually takes place in a relationship of two people, whether intimate or not? Almost any reaction is recorded in the brain, consciously or at a deeper level, especially those that are painful or pleasurable. This recording goes on from childhood until death. This record slowly builds up an image or picture which each person has of himself. If one is married or lives with another, for a week or for years, an image is formed about the other; the hurts, the irritations, the harsh words, the flatteries, the sensual responses, the intellectual appreciations, the companionship and tenderness, the imagination of fulfilment and cultural associations. These form the varying images that are awakened under different circumstances. Again, from actual physical relations, these images distort or deny a profound relationship of love and compassion with its intelligence.

'Then how or in what manner can these images not be formed?'

Are you not putting a wrong question, sir? Who is it that prevents? Is it not another image or idea that is putting the question? Are you not still working with images, from one to the other? Such inquiries lead nowhere. When one is hurt or wounded psychologically, from childhood on, the consequences of that hurt are obvious: fear of further hurts, withdrawal by building a wall around oneself, further isolation, and so on, a process of neuroticism. If and when one is aware, observes these wounds, the conflicts, then one instinctively demands how one can prevent being hurt. The ultimate image is the I, the self—capital 'S' and the small 's'. When one grasps the full significance of why the brain and thought form these images, the truth of why these images exist, that very perception dispels all the formation of images. This is the ultimate freedom.

'What is the reason the brain or thought form images?'

Is it for security? To be safe from danger? To be certain, to avoid confusion? Whatever small part of the brain is functioning, to function well, efficiently, it must feel certain, safe. Whether that certainty or security is an illusion or an invention of thought, as faith or belief, it is not actuality; it is of no importance as long as that limited part of the brain feels safe, assured, certain. In this illusion, we live. With the images, such as nationalism and the images in all the temples of the world, man lives and carries on with conflict, pleasure and sorrow. The forming of these images has no end. But when you perceive that they cast shadows on our actual lives, and so prevent profound relationship between each other, and that cloud, that tree and those children, then only can there be love.

August 11, 1981

Beauty is dangerous. Standing on that hill, one saw three hundred miles of the Himalayas, almost from horizon to horizon with its deep, dark valleys, peak after peak with everlasting snow, not a village, house or hut in sight. The sun was touching the highest peaks, and the roseate glow was spreading to the lower peaks, then all of a sudden the whole continuous range was afire. It was as though they were afire from within, aglow with incredible intensity. The valleys became darker, and the silence was absolute. The earth was breathless in its splendour. As the sun rose from over the far eastern peak, the immensity, the utter purity of that majestic mountain seemed so close one could almost touch them; but they were many hundreds of miles away. And the day began. No wonder man has always worshipped those mountains; they are sacred, to be adored from afar. The ancients made gods of them, for there the heavenly ones made their abode. Now they are making them into ski runs, building hotels and swimming pools. But not there among those implacable and incorruptible snows. Beauty is imperishable and infinitely dangerous.

Leaving that impenetrable silence, the rocky trail followed a stream and passed through many varieties of pines and large deodars. The path became wide and covered with grass, and took many turns. It was a lovely morning, soft with the scent of rich forest, and it was becoming warm. In the trees close by was a group of monkeys with long tails and grey hairy bodies, their faces shiny in the morning sun. The babies were clinging to their mothers, and the whole group was quietly watching the solitary figure. They watched unmovingly, unafraid. Presently a group of *sannyasis*, monks, passed, going down to the same distant village, chanting. Their Sanskrit was precise and clear, indicating they were from the far south. Their hymn was to the morning sun who gave life to all things and whose benediction is on all living things. There were eight of them, three or four quite young, all with shaven heads and clad in saffron robes, controlled, with downcast eyes, not looking at the great trees, the thousand flowers and the soft green hills; for beauty is dangerous and distracting; desire may be aroused.

The villagers were preparing their morning meals, and the smell of wood fires was in the air. The children, freshly washed, were preparing for school with shouts and laughter. Amidst the usual noise of a village was a sense of sad weariness. It had its temple and its priest, the believers and the unbelievers.

It is odd how the priests, from time beyond memory, have conditioned the human brain to have faith, to believe, to obey. They were the scholars, the teachers, the law. By their conduct, noble and responsible, they were the social guardians, upholders of tradition. Through fear, they controlled the kings and the people. At one time they were outside, apart from society so that they could

guide it, morally, aesthetically, religiously. They gradually
became the interpreters between gods and man. They had
power, status and the vast wealth of the temples, churches
and mosques. In the East, they covered their bodies in
simple, distinct coloured cloth. In the West, their ritual
garments became more and more symbolic, more and
more expensive. Then there were those simple monks
in monasteries and palaces. The religious heads, with
their plutocracy, held the people in faith, dogma, rituals
and words. Superstition, guile and hypocrisy became the
coin of all organised religions of the East and the West.
And that which is most sacred went out of the window,
however beautiful the window be.

So man has to begin again to discover that which is
eternally sacred, never to be caught by interpreters, priests,
gurus, or by the peddlers of meditation. You have to be a
light to yourself. That light can *never* be given by another,
however respected by tradition, or by any philosopher or
psychologist. Freedom is to stand alone, unattached and
unafraid, free in the understanding of desire which breeds
illusion. There is vast strength in being alone. It is the
conditioned programmed brain that is never alone, for
it is filled with knowledge. That which is programmed,
religiously or technologically, is always limited. This
limitation is the major factor of conflict.

Beauty is dangerous for a man of desire.

August 12, 1981

There is a tree at least several hundred years old on the bank of the wide river; it is full of leaves, every branch covered with them, sparkling in the light of morning, each leaf aflutter in the breeze. The river was very wide, deep with flowing water, crystal clear. Parrots, kingfishers, flycatchers and other birds were always more active in the mornings and evenings. The bright green parrots were noisiest, screeching from one tree to another in their zigzag flight. The flycatchers in their sparkling blue were never noisy, but still on a branch. Suddenly they flew high and plunged into the water. The green flycatchers were on the nearest trees, bright golden green.

The river made a golden path as the sun rose over the trees on the other bank. As it climbed, the waters of the river came to life, dancing, and the ripples chased one another; it was an endless game they played all the day long, only to come to rest as the sun went down in the west. There were small boats going up and down the river, full of villagers singing and sometimes strangely, sadly quiet. It is a fascinating river and, as all great rivers, sacred. Rivers have no names but are great flowing waters; man gives them names and so makes them local and so makes them their own.

Every morning, a monkey, brown and small, was on the topmost branch of that old tree, warming itself and looking over his domain. Then after a few minutes it would disappear, to appear again the next morning. We watched each other regularly; it always looked to see if one was looking up. One year later, it was no longer there. That old tree was very beautiful; it dominated all others. It was the home of many birds. The small screech owls lived there, and in the evening they would come out with their shrill rattling screech, taking short flights until it became quite dark, but one could hear them during the night. And in the morning, there they were, sitting close together and warming themselves. Then they disappeared for the day.

One used to sit under that old tree before the sun was up, in the silent dawn when the world was silent. The large trunk was massive, peaceful, the life of several hundred years. One sat there utterly still, without a single movement of thought, without time, in utter emptiness, with the essence of absolute order and so of the universe. Then the sun was among the leaves, with dappled shadows. The leaves were awaking. Each year it offered the silence of trees, and each year it was older and slowly dying. When one came back, it was losing its leaves but was still beautiful. Two years later it was gone, and in its place was a small plant of the same kind, protected and cared for. All nature is beautiful in its death.

Man has always been concerned with death, in every culture, in every civilisation, worshipping it or frightened of it, or considering it as a means to a greater or fuller life, carrying over the things possessed in this life. Your dog, your chattels and even your wife if you loved her. Or there is only this life, and death is total annihilation. Live righteously and be rewarded for it in the next life. Believe this, have faith, and heaven is open; but if that programmed faith is denied, then of course there is the other place. Man has conjured up so many beliefs, so many rewards and punishments; but the final ending is always there, do what you will.

'I have been assiduously studying your teachings for some years, attending your talks whenever possible, and I have a collection of your dialogues with professors and psychiatrists. As a solicitor, I am fairly logical, and I hope objective. My father, who was also a solicitor, died some years ago. I had a family. My son was driving with his mother, and a lorry ran into them; they were both killed instantly. It was a great shock to me, and it has affected me deeply. I feel rather strongly guilty. I will spare you the details of my agony and loneliness, the emptiness of life and the meaninglessness of that accident. I have come to you to talk about the significance of death. I would like to spend some considerable time, sir, being with you and talking over with you this terrible misery.'

We were silent for several minutes, for he was deeply moved. Life is a sad business, seemingly without significance and long-lasting.

'I am sorry to break down; it has been a lonely, desperate fight. I know and deeply feel that you understand all this. Please let us talk about it, not the accident but about the ending of life.'

Could we look together at the fact of death, the death of every living thing? One hopes you will not mind, though this accident has been quite recent, to observe how man has faced death. He has invented every means of escape from the inevitable end, ever seeking some form of continuity, some comforting explanation, rational or not—the avoidance of the whole subject. You must surely be aware of all this. Can we put aside all this and be wholly concerned with what death is and who it is that dies? Please, sir, this not a cruel question, and one hopes you will understand. Who is it that dies and what is death?

'I am doing my best, and please be patient. If you went into it step by step, I would be most grateful.'

Who is it that dies? The father, the son, the wife, the brother, who are separate from me, separate individuals in name, form, characteristics, capacity and so on; individuals with their peculiar idiosyncrasies, biologically and psychologically, inwardly. Each one of us thinks and acts distinctly and different from another. We think each one of us has his own destiny, his own future, freedom of choice, freedom to act independently. In our attachments, be it to the family, to the experience or the convictions, there is this feeling and certainty that assures each one of us that we are individuals, separate and deeply unique. This is the tradition, the religious sanction, the law and the education.

'So far I follow.'

But are we individuals, though a thousand years say we are? Our souls, our being, our very existence is separate, unique—is this so? The so-called separate human beings throughout the world stand on a common ground of sorrow, pain, boredom, loneliness, anxiety, insecurity, perpetual conflict, with occasional joy and the pleasure and grief of all mankind. This is the fundamental basis of all mankind, East or West. Our whole consciousness is made up of this, the collective, the particular group, the family. The content of our consciousness is made up of all those: the beliefs, the faiths, the ideals and so on.

'I am with you so far, perhaps intellectually. Your arguments so far appear logical and observable. Please proceed.'

It is not only to be grasped intellectually, but it is an actual fact that all human beings are deeply, fundamentally similar, though their culture and education may vary. The human being is violent, ready to kill for his ideals, for his territory, for his gods. This is the common background of all human beings. Of course, there are rare exceptions. The consciousness of one is the consciousness of all. You are the entire humanity. You are the world and the world is you. This is not an ideal to be achieved, a utopia to be striven for. This is an actual living reality, not a concept put together by experiences and thought. It is so. When one actually realises this, what then is an individual? Does it actually exist, or is it an illusory concept, a tradition which we have accepted without doubt, without question? All religions have maintained the individuality, with a separate soul and so on. This is one of the causes of division which must invariably bring about conflict between other human beings and within himself. Where there is division between nations, religions, beliefs, there must be conflicts, wars, every form of cruelty. This is not an opinion, but it is a law.

'Sir, would you mind my asking what happens to my son after death?'

This a question almost everyone asks without considering it deeply. Who it is that dies?

'Is he swallowed up by the common consciousness? Does he no longer exist? This is hard to accept. I cannot deeply feel this to be so. I loved my son and my wife, they are there in the house in my thoughts, and it is so terribly cruel to consider that they have become part of the total human consciousness. It is a horrible idea.'

Forgive me, sir, to point out that a few minutes ago we both seemed to agree about the logic and the sanity of the ground on which all human beings stand, the ground of sorrow, loneliness, anxiety and so on. This is the content of every so-called individual consciousness. This content is similar, common to all mankind. You see this objectively, dispassionately, to be a fact, don't you?

'Dispassionately, that is the cruel difficulty. It is a marvellous concept intellectually, but in my heart I don't feel it; it still clings to my son and wife as separate and distinct human beings.'

Again there is this division between the intellectual comprehension and the emotional attachment, thus engendering endless conflict. Why is there this division?

'It is fairly obvious. I am attached to the image I have of my son and that of my wife. These images are real, they are there, as association and memory. I can almost hear them talking, the tone of their voices. It is so sadly and painfully clear.'

The actuality of past memories, the actuality of the common ground and remembrances of things past—these remembrances are also, in a way, actual; this actuality is something that is over and gone. We cling to that which is gone, which has vanished. The real we reject, but we hold on to that which is dead memory. Please realise that one is not being cruel. That which has gone has become more important than *what is*; as long as we remain in this field of consciousness, with its illusory individuality, ever becoming, there must be sorrow and infinite loneliness.

'It is so hard, so painful to give up all the cherished, dear memories. I almost cry in letting them go. So sorrow remains.'

No sir. Sorrow exists as long as the content of consciousness continues. Perception of the truth of this is the ending of sorrow.

'What then is there? If I let go all the bundle of memories, what then is there, sir?'

Abandon them entirely and see what happens.

'You will say love, compassion and intelligence, an indivisible movement. May I be with you a little longer?'

August 14, 1981

There is a rickety old bridge over a small stream. It is made of tall bamboo tied together with pieces of what appears to be string, and clay from the banks of the stream. One has to be rather careful in crossing over this contraption, for there are large holes in it. This muddy stream below joins the wide river and there the pilgrims come to bathe, men and women, for where the narrow waters meet the wide flowing river is sacred. There the old and the young bathe in their everyday clothes, which become dry in the sun as they slowly wander back home. Over this temporary bridge, to be washed away when the rains come, the villagers pass with milk cans on their bicycles, the women carrying on their heads bundles of wood, hay, vegetables and whatever their villages produce. Early in the morning, these poor villagers cross the stream on their dangerous bridge coming from the city, cheerfully chattering. It is a sad life, meagre and painful, but they seem to be always chattering and laughing.

One day a group was building another bridge just upstream, with stout, freshly cut green bamboo, with precision and care, the long bamboo green and bright in the sun, tied to firm stakes to prevent anyone falling over. This new bridge was a work of art, so simple and strong, with steps leading down to it on both sides of the stream. Some important person was to cross it with his entourage. The builders began early in the morning and were finished long before midday. The floor of the bridge was smooth and firm, without any holes, unlike the other. The workers waited, and the villagers gathered to watch. Presently the religiopolitical leader, with a very large following, crossed the garlanded bridge without looking up or down the stream, unaware of the other bridge, and was greeted on the far bank by a large crowd, which took him up the road. They were all chattering but not laughing. Before the evening, the beautiful bridge was gone. There was no trace of it, not even the steps. The other bridge remains, collecting toll from all who cross it. One almost had tears in one's eyes.

After leaving the bridge and the filthy village, and going far north among the great mountains, one stayed at a house. It was an isolated house with large, neglected gardens, full of weeds, with one or two roses in bloom. It was an odd house, with large rooms, empty save for an old bed and an older chair. There was no bathroom but a tap of running water, no toilet and nothing convenient. The windows had no glass, and there were several holes in the floor. Letters used to disappear, and one wondered why. Then we discovered some blue letter paper stuck in one of the holes. The rats were taking care of them. Within a week, the bulbuls were eating raisins out of one's hand. They were insatiable; they would sit on the window bars and call. They were beautiful birds, black with top feathers, the shape of their heads like all birds, symmetrical and as though well-polished.

One morning doing some kind of yoga, there was a
large shadow at the window. It was a large wild monkey,
black-faced with a long, curved tail, its body covered with
soft grey hairs. It was probably wondering why that human
was so still. It stretched out a long arm with an open hand.
We held hands together for some time, looking at each
other in wonderment, without any sense of fear. It was
the most wonderful hand that one held, long-fingered,
extraordinarily soft, pliable, narrow and warm. Only
the palm was rough. It didn't want to let go, but time
intervened and it vanished over the roof, not saying a word
of goodbye.

It was a lovely morning after days and days of rain,
with the clear blue skies of high altitudes, the air
cleansed of the dust of summer, and there was glory in
the land. Down in the valley, pilgrims by the hundreds
were slowly coming up a narrow path. They were from
all over the country, some in heavy boots and others in
bare feet, some in warm, heavy clothes and others in
freshly washed white cloth; the women in bright dresses
and the older ones in fawncoloured silks or plain cottons.
There were monks in saffron robes with long canes, and
there were grown-up boys and girls. There was not much
talk as the path was steep. As they reached a fairly wide,
level place, they all came to rest, before continuing on
their long climb of many days, eventually reaching the
high point of their pilgrimage, a temple among the rocks
and caves.

This kind of pilgrimage goes on all over the world, perhaps not so strenuous and dangerous as this one; some of the pilgrims had crawled on their hands and knees. But it is the same spirit, whether in the East or West, the same sense of dedication and devotion. In different and varied forms, this pilgrimage has been going on century after century, perhaps not so often in these more sophisticated times. Now people go to nightclubs, gambling places and resorts.

We were quietly watching with a friend this seemingly endless procession, when he said rather hesitantly, 'I have been on such a pilgrimage, taking vows, with every form of carnal abstinence, to an image in a faraway temple. The image is said to be thousands of years old. When I see all those people, I am, with them, full of inexpressible mystery and abandonment, leaving behind all responsibility. I was like a soldier following orders I was following the call of that image, obeying as the soldier does, drunk with the idea of patriotism; and I drank with devotion to that image. We are all mad, sometimes sane and at other times insane, driven by ideas, hate or devotion. I am sane now, perhaps, up here away from my work and with you. Why are we so deeply committed to symbols and images?'

Image-making by the hand or the brain is with all of us—the flag, the image in the temple or church, the image of ourselves and others, the images of the foreigner, the barbarian, and so on. Why do we cultivate these pictures and symbols, and who is the cultivator? 'Who is the cultivator?' is a far more important question than what he cultivates. What is the machinery, the entity that conceives and projects the image? Is it desire, is it thought, or a totally different factor? If it is desire, seeking satisfaction in security, in possession of things or in ideas of perfection, of becoming successful in the world or in the so-called spiritual existence, who is the maker of images? If it is desire, what is the source of it?

One can find the beginning of a river by following it up through towns, valleys, into the hills, and so on. So one can find the beginning of desire. There are several streams that give volume to the water to the river. So there are several factors that make up desire, however strong and passionate it be. The objects of desire may vary, they may be noble or decadent, but desire is constant. What is desire? The major factor is the sensation of touch, smell, sight. This sensation is either partial, or all the sensory responses act together. When they act wholly together, the driving energy of desire withers away, but we hardly ever, except in a great crisis, respond wholly. The partial response is the problem.

'I have never heard you say to respond with all our senses. Would you mind explaining what you mean?'

Do you see that hill with its waterfall? Do you see it only with your eyes? Do you hear it only with the hearing of the ears? Do you only smell those thousand wildflowers? If you do, it is only a partial awakening of the senses; but to observe that hill, the waterfall and the flowers with all your senses fully awakened, then there is that quality of an integral whole. That perception is absolute order.

'I am not sure I understand the depth of your statement. I am sure you don't mean only sensuality—the total awakening of attention is entirely another matter. Please continue.'

We are talking about desire, the objects of desire made by thought or by hand, and how desire arises. Desire is always partial, for it is never satisfied; there is always measure in it: the better, the more. All action born of desire must inevitably be partial and so brings about conflict. As we were asking, what is desire with its energy and passion? Without sensation, there is no desire. How does desire arise from sensation? First there is seeing, visual perception, then there is contact, touch, then sensation. Then comes a wholly different response, the response of thought. Thought creates the image of you in that car or suit. When thought creates the image, at that second desire is born. Religious people, monks the world over, try to escape from it in multiple ways, or try to suppress it, but are always burning with it, never understanding or investigating the movement of desire. To desire food, clothing and shelter is natural and necessary but psychological desires breed problems and confusion.

Sensations too, like sensitivity, are natural, sane, but when thought comes in with its images, its pictures, then trouble begins with its pain and misery.

'Why does thought create images, the whole world of imagination? Can one ever be free of these? They may be useful for the artist or poet but in everyday life, don't we also need them; aren't they part of our existence? Without images, what would we be? The very idea is frightening.'

Knowledge is the image. Knowledge is the basis of one's life. Knowledge saves lives, but knowledge also destroys. Knowledge can be measured, and so ignorance exists. Ignorance and knowledge are inseparable, and this invites conflict. We esteem knowledge and forget the dark shadow of ignorance. Knowledge is the vast experience of humanity, stored in books and in the brain, which is the timeless recording machine, the inventor of gods, atom bombs, tortures and the rituals of worship. Knowledge breeds fear, pleasure and sorrow. To know is to suffer. Man hopes to reach heaven, peace through suffering, which is knowledge. You know your wife and child; that is why you suffer. Knowledge is the word, the form, the remembrances, the image. But the word is not the living person but the remembrances. The image remains, and that is the torture, the pain, the utter loneliness. Beauty is not the image or that hill with flowing waters. Knowledge of all that is not *that*, nor are all the remembrances of your wife and son. It is not harshness that is saying all this.

Why does thought put together the many images about oneself and about others, intimate or not? Is it a form of security, assurance, to be certain? When you have an image about another, there is safety in being. It establishes a routine, complacency. You *know* your wife, and that is that. These images formed about each other over days or years are the causes of conflict between human beings, between nations, races and classes. Can the formation of these images come to an end?

'It seems very hard not to form images. I forced myself, willed not to have them, but it is almost impossible.'

This makes for another question. Who is the controller, the will that wishes to end the making of images? Is the image separate, different from the controller, the maker of the image? Are they not one and the same? The controller and the controlled are the same. The observer and the observed are one. It is thought that divides, brings about fragmentation, for thought itself is limited; it is the outcome of knowledge which in itself is a fragment. When you perceive the truth of this, then only will the brain cease to record, the image-making end. The brain is constantly recording, necessarily and unnecessarily. It is necessary to record where one lives, the language, skills and so on, but is it necessary to record psychologically?

'Can the image-making naturally stop without any compulsion, without any effort?'

Only when there is an insight into the nature and structure of thought, who is the imagemaker. Then only is there an end to the making of images. Insight is without any motive and is complete attention.

August 16, 1981

In the high Sierras, there was not a soul in sight. One climbed up and up a stony path among scattered pines. It was a clear warm day, almost hot. It was a day for climbing; there was a slight breeze which carried the warm smell of the pines. One had left below the huge sequoias, the enormous redwood trees Native Americans call the silent ones. And they are silent, motionless, reaching to the heavens. To be among them is to lose all sense of time. They were there long before history. The silent ones had endured with immense dignity. Leaving them, the rough path went up a steep hillside away from all noise and man. There were no buildings at that altitude, and the silence was absolute. The breeze had stopped, and far down below were the lakes, the rushing streams and the cottages of the National Park. It was a magnificent sight; the Sierras never seemed to end, and far away there were snow-capped mountains, almost lost in a mist. They seemed to be floating in the air, insubstantial and untouchable. One felt the immensity of vast space and lost to all reality.

As one came down on an equally difficult stony path, there was a small open space, green and fresh. As one came round a bend, there was a huge, dark grizzly bear with four cubs, the size of large cats. The mother pushed them up a tree; they furiously climbed and one could hear the noise of their claws on the bark. The mother was barring the way,

firm on its four furry legs, facing one. We looked at each
other without any movement. We stood there, unafraid,
and presently the bear turned and went on her way. One
never realised the danger of the situation; it dawned only
when the incident was related to the forest ranger. He was
furious, pointing out that the bear could have mauled one
to pieces, or killed one, especially with her cubs there. But
the huge bear with its small cubs, the floating snow-capped
mountains and the vast stillness, wiped away all fear
and danger.

Man has always sought truth—not the legendary truth,
the truth of books or the utterances of the priest. Of course,
the politicians will never find it nor the politico-religious
and certainly not the traditionalists. In spite of them all,
man had sought truth. In seeking it, he has been snared
by philosophies, by the sacred hymns, by all the romantic
absurdities of thought. He has looked and searched in
all the distant places, in all the shrines in all manmade
structures. It has always eluded him, except for those
fortunate few. What is truth, and what is reality? One
can understand what reality is, but the other is not to be
understood by the brain with its senses or reason or
logic—reality is all the things that that has put together,
but the forest, the tiger, that black dog are not made by
thought; the word is, but not the stream. They are realities
but not the product of thought. The gods in all the temples
of the world are realities invented by thought and so by
hand. They are realities, like illusions and ideals.

'The things of thought and nature are two different phenomena,' a visitor said. 'That is fairly clear and acceptable. Are you saying that that which is not thought is truth? You have said the things of thought and thought itself is reality, and in itself it is not and never will be sacred. That again is fairly comprehensible to any intelligent person.'

One is not so sure that this is accepted by so-called intelligent man. If he did, the temples and churches would be emptied overnight. It is very hard and dangerous to realise, not verbally or intellectually, that thought with its delusions and images, its logic and ideals, is very limited and will ever be so. Peace cannot be the product of thought, however it might organise for it. Peace cannot be bought through prayer, discipline, or through any organisation, religious or secular. To have peace, one must live peacefully.

'What you are saying is almost impossible to actually live in the modern world. Our very existence is a series of struggles and endless conflicts. We are caught in this everlasting turmoil until we die.'

We are educated to strive, to become. This learning is the very core of our lives: to become 'spiritually' and to succeed in the outer world. Achievement is rewarded. Truth is not a reward; that which is, which is nameless, is not to be achieved. It is not there at the end of long, strenuous discipline, sacrifice or abstinence.

'Then what is one to do? If none of these will ever lead to that, then there is nothing to be done.'

Please, do understand that thought cannot, do what it will, comprehend or realise that. Let us go on to explore the incapacity of thought, though it is capable of building dams, computers, rapid communications and so on.

First of all, truth is not a fixed point; it is not static; it cannot be measured by words; it is not a concept, an ideal to be achieved. But look what human beings have done, what thought has conceived. The ancients of the part of the world now called India devised three main paths to that measureless—the path of knowledge, the path of action and the path of devotion. They said all these would eventually lead to that. These three ways of life are based on different capacities, different temperaments; romantic, emotional, active, intellectual. There is the Christian way, the Buddhist and Islamic, with different beliefs, faiths and dogmas. Thought is the origin of all these delusions, separative and so conflicting, destructive.

'I see this is the actual state of the world in which we live. One could argue against these actualities, but the arguments would be merely dialectical, opinion against opinion. All right, then what next?'

When one truly grasps the utter limitation of thought, that it cannot fathom the immeasurable, that thought is functioning from only a small part of the whole brain, and our senses are not acting as a whole, the very profound realisation of these facts brings about the action of that energy which is not the energy of memory and conflict. This is insight. The scientist, the artist, the poet, have partial insight—one hopes they will forgive us for stating this. Only the truly religious man has this total, complete insight.

August 18, 1981

The miracle of a waterfall, of a tree, of a cloud! Man is captivated by miracles, some extraordinary happening, unnatural, unexplained. A flower is the greatest miracle in the world; it is an everyday, common thing. The birth of a child, the jet engine and the glory of a cathedral are all miracles but are a common sight, and we pass them by with a glance and passing memory. We want something beyond reason and its explanation. The laying-on of hands, a cure without medicine or surgery, healing from a distance—there are so many forms of these phenomena. Thought is ever probing into the mystery of the unexplained. There are miracle mongers, but they are not the miracle. There are those who levitate, defying gravity, and there are those who try to teach how to levitate at so much a lesson. Those who teach have not themselves denied gravity. Scepticism is healthy, and doubt sweeps away all illusions. This, in itself, is a miracle. One has done many of these things, and then what? To make a name for oneself, which is silly. To gather money in the name of religion, sanctity and status, is childish, utterly immature.

Some of us were sitting on a veranda in the evening; the sun had set, it was cool with a fresh breeze coming in from the north, from the far away snows. None of us were drinkers. There were eight of us, four professors from the university, two very well-known scholars and a layman. We were talking about the nature of the mind, its deceptions,

illusions and the tricks it plays. There were some natural
contradictions, but on the whole there was general
agreement, passionate and desultory. It was quite light still,
and one could see the roses in full bloom. It was a pleasant
evening, in spite of the talk. There was silence for a long
time, quiet, withdrawn. The shapes of the trees against the
darkening sky were marvellous.

Into this silence, the gentle hesitant voice of the domestic
broke in. It said there was a stranger waiting to see us. He
looked like a beggar, with very little on, rather shy and
awkward. He said he would like to show us something.
Pointing to me, he continued that he would not mesmerise
'as you are a holy religious man', and since the others were
there, there would be no hypnosis. The others were smiling
and wondering what it was all about. There was a large bed
of roses around which there was a carriageway. The man sat
on the other side of the rose bed, away from the seven steps
and the veranda. He was a small man, very thin, almost
emaciated. He asked for a newspaper to be brought. It was
then folded in the middle, and again, one side over the
other, and it was put on one of the steps. The man never
touched it; it was always in the hands of one of the group
until it was on the step. The man asked us to keep our eyes
on the folded newspaper. He had closed his eyes. Some of
us were watching the paper, and others were looking at the
man. Then as the eight of us watched the paper, it began to
get smaller and smaller, and suddenly it totally disappeared.
It wasn't there on the step. It wasn't a stage trick; the man

took no money, but one offered food which he took. He explained that he had taken a vow to the goddess who had given this gift never to touch money, but to accept cloth for his body, and food. We never saw him again. There was much speculation after he left. There was no doubt of its disappearance nor of it being a conjurer's trick. We were not hypnotised; we were a rather sceptical group, and some of us have witnessed such strange phenomena. We were not gullible people.

There are miracles but not for sale. Those who really have this gift never seek publicity, never do it for money, and they never claim to be religious or spiritual. Others make of them what they want them to be. But they avoid them; they certainly don't want followers in the name of God. They are not holy men; they are ordinary people with a certain capacity.

It is strange how man pursues the occult, the gurus, those who give you, through drugs and other means, uncommon experiences. Books are written about it, strange beings in faraway places who instruct and guide; yogis who are making enormous sums of money. Money, power, status, and of course, arrogance, are the basis of those who have something to sell in the so-called world of spirituality. Man, dissatisfied with ordinary sensuous experiences, craves for super, mysterious experiences, through drugs, through the repetition of mantras, through yogic exercises and so on. None of these are really worth the effort, the expense, the following. Repetition is vain, whether in the temple, church or mosque; these rituals are utterly meaningless. The mantra, whose true meaning is to meditate upon not-becoming and to put away all self-centred activity, can be bought and may be repeated a thousand times. This makes the brain duller but is not the ending of the self. Through certain words or through drugs, rituals, worship or prayers, you do not end the turmoil of the self.

The greatest mystery is yourself; the story of yourself, whose book you alone can read. The commentators, those who explain what you are talking about, themselves have their own problems and confusion. The story of yourself is the story of the entire humanity. To read that book as it is actually written, without interpreting it, without motive or direction, becomes the only challenge. The external world, the society of which you are, is rapidly degenerating, full of danger and war. Each one is wholly responsible for this and totally responsible for himself, for one's thoughts and actions. To read this book of mystery, there must be freedom. The schoolboy is free to read a book on any subject, but he is distracted; playful but nevertheless curious. If you are not curious about yourself or are easily, superficially satisfied, then drugs, the endless meaningless ritual, the books all about yourself, and the distant instructors, whose disciples write about them, will be your distraction. You then become utterly irresponsible.

So learn about yourself diligently. You can read the whole book of yourself at a glance, or read page by page, chapter after chapter, until the end of your days. Time is not a factor in this learning.

August 19, 1981

In the zoo, against green hills and trees, were two
marvellous tigers. They were seemingly small but had
imposing dignity and strength. Presently they lay down
in the grass, their heads towards us. There were very few
people about, and a strange communication seemed to take
place between the watcher and the watched. But who was
the watcher, those two or the other? This communication
continued until some children came, shouting and
laughing. Then the tigers got up and withdrew among the
trees. They seemed to have such enormous energy, like a
walking dynamo.

We waste our energy by misusing it, by constant thought
and occupation. Even in sleep the brain is active. We have
incredible energy. See what we have done in the world:
building and destroying; climbing the highest peaks and
going down into deep water; the jet passing overhead at
great height and speed; giving birth and killing; the striving
and the plotting. Outwardly we have achieved great things,
polluting and preserving. Inwardly we are everlastingly
occupied with ourselves, our problems fears and sorrows,
striving, driving, ever in conflict, with never a moment
when the brain is utterly quiet, nor the senses. This
perpetual occupation until one dies is a waste of energy.
Occupation, with God or the kitchen, noble or ignoble, is
the same; the brain being busy with its own existence is a
waste of energy.

Emptiness is supreme energy. Emptiness is without measure; emptiness is space. We are frightened to be nothing, to be free, free from all occupation. To be psychologically concerned, occupied with the means of livelihood, the inward specialisation, the inward conceit of discipline, the inward achievement, is a waste of energy. One may listen or read about all this and strive not to be occupied, but that very effort is a wastage of energy. When there is insight, not partial, then only is there that vast energy of emptiness.

For most of us, to be something or become something is all-important. It is so inherent in us, and the very idea to be nobody is horrifying. All that which we have done, physically or otherwise, is to identify ourselves.

All the great temples and cathedrals were built by people who have not left their names to posterity. It may be the modern craze to seek identification; that is to be or become somebody. Even after death, the continuity of the self is comfortingly important. The self needs identification; the part is significant; it thinks it establishes an infinite continuity. The self is a verbal structure of memories, pleasures and pain. The remembrances and future anticipations and hopes limit the capacity of the brain and hence breed sorrow. All knowledge is ever in the shadow of ignorance. The insight into the nature and structure of the self is the ending of sorrow. Only then is there love, compassion and intelligence.

BROCKWOOD PARK

August 23, 1981

He was working on one of the most expensive European cars. He was a very good mechanic, trained at its makers, very capable; and there were other expensive cars he was looking after. We had known each other for many years; when one was stripping an engine, he came to help. His capacity was remarkable; he used to go out to sea on his little sloop, and he played the flute. He taught one to play it, but there were other things to do. His garage was close to a seaside resort and had plenty of work to do. It was in a valley surrounded by hills, and they were green with plenty of rain. A single raindrop contained all the rivers, and every bank was its playground, like the cities and the green pastures; it is behind all dams and in all the lakes, and of course the sea. What a wonder it is to see a parched land turn green almost overnight after the rains begin, the first fresh green shoot so tender, translucent, delicate. All the grass of the world is in one blade. The cattle became fatter, and the villagers were smiling. Every leaf was washed clean and was sparkling in the soft morning. The little stream became a torrent, only to die to its former trickle in the heat of summer. This is the life of that stream year after year, summer after summer. So life goes on.

Through study, discipline, training and application, it is possible to have capacity, as it is through some form of experience. Capacity can be learning capacity, based on knowledge and so limited. An architect draws a plan for a house not only from his knowledge, but also from some kind of inspiration. Experience, knowledge and some other factor give that capacity necessary to be a surgeon or a master carpenter. Capacity becomes almost mechanical when a deeper factor does not enter into it. It inherently has its own energy but even that factor is limited through specialisation.

'What are you trying to say, sir? What you are saying is fairly obvious.'

Must capacity be grounded in experience and knowledge? Is it a process of time, inherited? If it is, it becomes mechanical, rather tiresome. There is a capacity which is not of time and knowledge. The capacity that insight brings is not of memory, and so it is the expression of the whole.

'What do you mean by that word insight of which you have spoken often?'

Apart from the dictionary meaning, it is to perceive with
the whole of one's being without time-memory, in a flash,
the complete significance, say of capacity. It cannot be
willed, nor must there be a motive. The essence of insight
is freedom; freedom from all thought and reaction. Such
capacity born of insight can never become mechanical; it is
sane and logical. It is never personal. Insight is intelligence,
which is not yours or mine. Insight into a problem, say
sorrow, is its end. The small or the partial part of the
brain we use creates problems, and that same partial brain
is conditioned to solve problems, and so they multiply.
Insight is the activity of the whole of the brain.

'I more or less follow, but how can the whole of the
brain be awakened?'

First of all, there is no *how*, no method or a system.
There is no way, no path to it. Do you have an insight
of this, or are you arguing about it silently, inwardly? If
you really listen to what is being said, you will naturally
perceive the truth of it. It is this unhindered perception
that frees the brain from its conditioning. The clear,
unhindered perception is insight. It has its own energy and
non-mechanical capacity.

August 24, 1981

It was one of those cottages for summer visitors, with all that was necessary for a short visit. It was rather uncomfortable, small, with a kitchen and a bath. It was way up in the north in rather an isolated place, and the cottage was away from others. It was quiet in the forest, and at night there were the noises of small animals, and occasionally there was a thump as a big animal rubbed or knocked against the wood. It was quite cool at night and fortunately not too hot in the summer; at that latitude the sun was mild, with all those trees. It would snow in the coming winter. It was pleasant to be alone, away from the hustle and the dirt of towns, to be alone without talking or seeing anyone. To come up here was quite a business: train, then bus or car, and a walk. It was a beautiful place in the mountains and far away were the snow-covered peaks. There were good walks beside a fast-running torrent, or among the thick wood, and there was always the perfect blue sky and a thousand stars at night, close and brilliant in that clear air.

One had been there for some time when one day a group of monks in their saffron robes came rushing down the hill to the cottage. They were eager to talk, and some of them spoke English, fortunately. They said they had been to see a very holy man who was a man of great knowledge. He lived in a cave near to a small village. It took some days to get up there. He was alone, without any disciples around him, and he was known for his knowledge. On their way down they heard about the occupant of the cottage, and so here they were. They were quite young, except for one or two. The elders desired to have a dialogue, if possible. We were sitting in the shade on a thick layer of pine needles. They all had shaven heads, were scrupulously clean and polite. The older one started by asking, 'What is it to be alone and what is knowledge? Can the two exist together.'

One can never be alone and at the same time be full of knowledge; they contradict each other, don't they?

'The man we went to see is a hermit, and we wanted to learn from him the knowledge he had acquired through many years of meditation. Before he withdrew from the world, he was a great scholar, respected and was already regarded as a saint.'

Knowledge can be transmitted verbally or through the written word. The very word indicates that which is known, that which can be learnt. To be versed in the sacred books, as they are called, is knowledge of a certain type; the knowledge of mathematics, physics and so on, is another. There are many different categories of knowledge. Is the knowledge you went to learn, if one may ask, sacred, something secret?

'There are those who know and those who are ignorant. We do not know, so we seek.'

193

What is it that you do not know, sir?

'Knowledge of the supreme, that which is.'

What do you mean by the words *to know*? The carpenter knows how to make a table; he knows because he has watched, studied the nature of the wood; he is skilful with his hands. Because of his experience, he knows how to make a chair or table. So can you know that which is supreme?

'Yes. We can learn from another who experienced the highest.'

Are you saying, sir, that which is supreme can be put into words? The word is never the actual; the word is a symbol. The word *sky* is not the actual sky. Words have become very important to us; we almost live on them.

'But we follow the path of knowledge. To us the knowledge of the highest principle, Brahma, is our pursuit; knowing that is the answer to all our human problems.'

It is not possible to experience that or to know that. Who is the experiencer, the one who witnesses? Is he not the past, the accumulated memories? Knowledge is of time, the past. With a brain that is shaped and conditioned by the accumulations of a thousand yesterdays, you are trying to comprehend that which is timeless.

'I see what you are enunciating, but knowledge, of the universe and of oneself, has been the highest aim of man. Science is the investing of matter in this process; it has gathered formidable knowledge, both for good and evil.'

Knowledge is necessary at one level, and at another it becomes destructive. This has been the way of all civilisations and cultures. The truly religious must transcend this traditional, well-established and respectable pattern. The truly religious are the foundations of a new culture, a new society, not the politicians, not those who belong to established traditional organisations called religions, not the scientists, not the gurus.

We were all silent for a while. A bulbul, a black bird with a tuft on its head, which was becoming friendly, flew in, sat on the windowsill and joined us in that silence.

'What type of meditation do you practise?'

No system of meditation.

'Why?'

Following any method or system not only makes the brain dull but also makes it mechanical. The very word *practice* denies meditation. Meditation is not a gathering of knowledge but the ending of all knowledge. The self, the higher or the lower, the higher or lower consciousness, is the source and storehouse of knowledge.

'We would like to point out that meditation is necessary for self-discipline. Through meditation, we bring order in our lives to control our desires and emotions.'

Surely it is the other way round. First you put your house in order and then only perhaps meditation. If there is no order first, meditation may be a self-delusion or a form of self-hypnosis, the pursuit of some desired illusion. Bring order in your daily relationship with all living things, then only is there the awakening of the beauty of meditation.

That bird was still at the windowsill.

August 26, 1981

The cottage far up in the north among the great mountains
was reserved only for some high army people. By some
mistake or other, it was put at our disposal. You got to
it, tired and dirty, by a tediously long journey. It had
pleasant, green surroundings, but the cottage itself was
rather primitive and not very convenient. The local servant
was not too clean. The first thing was to get him clean, to
give him new clothes and to see that he was all right. The
weather was perfect, but there was in the air the feeling
of rain. You walked up the hill, past the heavy trees with
their deep shadows, round the bend to a narrow flat space.
There they were, those incredible mountains, range after
range, for miles, deep in silence with the early morning sun
on them. The undying grandeur and beauty of them drove
away all thought. You were the earth, the heavens and that
majesty.

Some days later, a man came to announce that in a
nearby village a tiger had killed a cow. You paid little
attention to it for you were occupied with your own
thoughts and to the odd corners it led you to. But towards
the evening you said to yourself that you would like to see
that tiger. So you walked down the hill, passing villages and
into the forest. It was a forest wild with creepers, bushes
and varieties of tall trees. As you went deeper in, it became
denser; the air was fresh with the smell of a thousand
things. You looked around, listening to the various noises

of the jungle, going further in. And suddenly there was complete silence; all the things of the earth seemed to hold its breath. There was danger; you felt it too. Your curiosity said to go a little further to see what is there, to see the animal in this wilderness. But the body refused to move an inch, even to move against the trunk of that tree so close by. It was not frightened but in no way could it be persuaded to move. It just stood there. And as suddenly, the whole forest woke up and all the birds, the things of the earth began their call before the night began. Then you too turned, making your way out of the forest.

As you passed a small clearing, you suddenly stopped for again there was a peculiar stillness, not of fear but as though you were being watched. You thought a deer or other animal close by was silently, warily aware of your presence. There was no living thing around you, and then you looked up. On the trees around that clearing were twenty or more big monkeys. Some of them had their babies clinging to them, and all were motionless. They looked down at you with great curiosity, totally unafraid. Presently they disappeared without any sound, and you went up to your cottage. You didn't see the tiger but saw those beautiful monkeys. It was a wonderful sight, the monkeys looking down upon you.

'I would like to ask you several questions if you have the time. The first one I would like to ask is, what is beauty? It is not an idle question. I happen to travel a great deal and have been to most of the important museums of the world. The modern painters don't mean much to me. I inherited one or two paintings of the old masters and I live with them. I picked up one of your books in an old bookshop and was impressed by what it contained. So my interest is not casual, and here I am to ask and perhaps have a dialogue. What has brought me to see you is in itself rather a curious affair, but that can wait.'

Why, if one may ask, do you ask what beauty is? Is it an abstract question, or after seeing so many paintings are you asking yourself what beauty is, to feel out, explore the depth and the essence of that feeling, fleeting or abiding? You must have naturally spent a great deal of time in those museums; does it take time to cultivate the appreciation of any beautiful painting?

'That is a good question. My father was some kind of artist. He was an amateur; he used to take me to art galleries and certain exhibitions. At first I was rather bored, but gradually my father began to educate me and my interest grew, and somehow passion crept into it. Yes, it was a matter of education, time.'

So you think time is necessary. Is that so? When you look at that wide green lawn, with that single cedar, does it take time to see that splendour? Or the loveliness of a rose? You respond to that immediately if you are in the least sensitive. Whereas you need to be educated to appreciate the depth and colour, how the grouping is. In religious painting, only figures mattered, and nature was neglected until recently. The response to the shadows on that bright green lawn is immediate, and the museums take time. Why? Is the love of beauty to be educated in a school? Is beauty comparative, one master against another? Is beauty made personal? Then it becomes good taste. Beauty is never personal; like intelligence, it doesn't belong to any artist, poet or carpenter.

'Are you saying, sir, that the relationship to nature is considerably different from that to painting, poetry and architecture? Are you stating that to see the beauty of manmade things needs education, and to see that of nature is a direct response?'

Are we not moving further and further away from nature? Are we not losing our direct relationship to it? Have not literature, paintings, television become more necessary? The symbol has far greater significance than actuality, has it not? The beauty of a picture and that of a tree are similar when you have not your relationship to nature. The escape from actuality is making us more and more superficial, fanciful, romantic.

'We can sit back and admire a picture in a museum or in our own house; we are city dwellers and so museums have assumed greater meaning. We are so conditioned by our own environment that we lose the beauty of the whole. Let us go back to my original question: what is beauty, the feeling of it, the state of the mind that perceives it? Is it the exhilaration and stimulation that comes with it?'

When you see the majesty of a great mountain, what is the state of the beholder? Is he not completely absorbed by it? For a second he has forgotten himself, his problems, worries, anxieties. He is entirely lost in front of its immensity. A child absorbed by a toy, as long as the toy is not broken, is no longer noisy; he is quiet, lost to his surroundings. Is it that for a period of time, the noisy self is absent? Is it that the greatness of something drives away the self? Is beauty the absence of the self? The complexity and implications of this are fairly obvious. Now the question is, can the self, not absorbed by something external like music or by some inward fancy, can this centre within its own narrow circle ever end?

'Is it to end through meditation, through control or discipline?'

Never can it end through some means, through any action. There is no means to the ending of it. The ending of the self is its own reality. When the self is, beauty is not. To comprehend, to have an insight into this truth is the ending of the self. Beauty is love, and love is beauty.

August 27, 1981

There was a procession along a very narrow road of
a small town in the rocky hills overlooking the blue
Mediterranean. Cactus of several species grew there. The
ancient Greeks had chosen the place, and there they had
built their small, lovely theatre, which was spoilt by the
Romans; they went in for grandeur and nearly destroyed
its beauty. It looked over the bay and the eversmoking
Aetna. How beautiful the morning was—the clear blue
spotless sky and the still blue sea. Aetna had erupted some
days ago with great flames of fire and lava, but today it
was peaceful and covered with snow. It was an enchanting
place, but now it was being ruined by tourists, with a big
hotel and all the rest of it.

The religious procession was long. There was the local
band, then, some distance back, the choir, then the priests
with their incense and chanting. Then came the images
carried by the local dignitaries, all dressed in black, followed
by the people of the little town, laughing and chattering,
and boys and girls shouting and running all over the place.
There were dogs too. It was a cheerful procession, full of
noise and fun, everyone in their best clothes. The sea was
still blue and silent, and Aetna was still smoking.

There was another procession, bearing a highly decorated
image with a crown, covered with many-coloured scarves.
Their music was pipes and drums. Some were dancing;

boys were doing gymnastics; some folded their hands and others were respectfully saluting the image. The procession was not very well organised; it would stop to reform in some kind of order. There was much shouting to keep in line or giving orders about something or other. It was religious but very noisy. The long avenue of trees looked down on this procession and were glad when it went along towards the rough sea. Very rarely was this sea quiet; it was restless, with high waves driven by winds. In the little wood, away from the strong breeze, it was quiet. There was that blessing of the evening.

He seemed to be a well-read man, clever and bright-eyed. 'I would like to have a good discussion with you about religion and the contemporary religions of the world. I think I am a religious man, at least a civilised man. I have studied much religious literature, some very superficial, some highly intellectual, some mystical. So, what is religion, a religious life? I happen not to belong to any sect or any established, traditional religions, let me add.'

If one may ask, is your concern in this discussion intellectual, merely to gather more information, out of curiosity?

'I am dissatisfied with my life the way I live, and I have always been interested in a religious life. At one time I nearly became a monk, but I found that it was an escape. I am serious in my inquiry. I would not waste your time, if I weren't.'

Let us then put aside beliefs, faith, dogmas, rituals, prayers and all those kinds of activities. One must be utterly free of these to have a clear, objective perception; subjective perception is generally rather deceptive. Any concept, however rational, objective or based on experience, is verbal and to be distrusted. Every form of experience is subjectively conditioned and hence limited and personal. The ideal is a projection of thought, away from *what is*.

'Sir, are you brushing aside, however sanely and rationally, all theories, speculations and interpretations? And of course all symbols.'

Interpretations are symbols, are they not? There must be complete freedom to be able to inquire, freedom from all conditioning, from being programmed. Freedom is not at the end of long strenuous effort and discipline but at the very first step of all serious inquiry.

'Isn't that asking a great deal?'

Otherwise conditioning perpetuates itself, and the past impedes any examination. You were asking, were you not, what religion is? The etymological meaning of *religion* is not clear, but we know more or less the significance of that word: leading a moral life, to be free of violence, not to kill and so on. But it is also much more than all this. To seek that which is most sacred, the nameless the eternal—the religious mind is diligently concerned with this. If both of us, even intellectually, agree to this, not superficially, then we can proceed with the question. Religion is not belief, dogmas, rituals or even prayers. It is not surrendering yourself to some principle, concept or symbol, and of course not to any human being. This is essential.

'You certainly have destroyed the very foundation of all religions and sects. But what part does will play in the search for the eternal?'

It has no place in a religious life. Will is the quintessence of desire. The movement of desire is to be understood and not be suppressed or controlled, for the controller is the very desire itself. The controller is the controlled. The understanding of desire is simple, and at the same time quite complex. The objects of desire constantly vary according to age and circumstances. Desire and discontent always go together with conflict. Desire for peace, for enlightenment or for money is constant; it is still desire under whatever name. Desire is a flow, a movement of sensation strengthened by thought with an image. Learning about the nature of desire brings about its own place and order, without suppression or escape. This is very important to understand a religious life, to have an insight into it. Freedom from attachment is necessary to learn about the depth and beauty of a religious life. Attachment corrupts. To be tied to any activity of thought must inevitably lead to misery.

'I depend on my knowledge; my brain is occupied with it. I have read so much, argued so much. Knowledge has become all-important to me. Must I let that go too?'

The self, the ego is the storehouse of knowledge. Knowledge is sorrow; knowledge is conflict and pain. Knowledge is time. Knowledge gives birth to thought. Knowledge is always limited. So knowledge is ever in the shadow of ignorance.

'Aren't you making a religious life extremely difficult?'

Explanations sound, and are, difficult, but it is necessary to go beyond the word and the explanation, for otherwise we remain at a very superficial level. To lead a religious life demands intelligence, not the cunning, calculating intelligence of thought.

'What do you mean by that word *intelligence*?'

The word is never the actual. Intelligence is born from love and compassion. They are not three separate activities but are one movement. This truth is perceived only when the self is not. The self hides behind righteous words, social work, power, belief, faith and prayer. Learning about the nature and structure of the self, the deep-rooted selfishness, is a part of religious life. Where the self is, beauty, truth is not.

August 28, 1981

There was space and quietness in the large field—no cattle, no sheep, no humans, but a single large tree. Even the birds weren't there; it was distant from other trees, too open, too dangerous. There were moles, safe in the earth. There was a path on one side of the field, covered with grass and wildflowers, little used and almost forgotten. In that enormous field, the solitary tree seemed to have great significance, not as a symbol but as a living reality. A symbol can represent anything one desires. A piece of rock can represent the whole universe, but it is not the universe. We live by words and symbols but that single tree is of the earth, the darkness and the light. Especially so when by chance you sit under it, breathing the same air, feeling the same earth, looking at the same sky.

The tree had a very large trunk, dark and ancient. It was full of leaves and cast a long shadow. There was a slight breeze, and every leaf was awake and dancing in the clear sunlight. It was not the contrived dance of man East or West but a dance of light; it was not sensuous but of grace. Before him, it was. A few ravens disturbed the silence, but the tree was not their home and after a great deal of cawing they left. With the evening there was greater silence and peace that seemed to descend upon the earth.

The streets were crowded, noisy, dirty, with the smell of a thousand people. The cars and the buses had to slow down. The shops were full of things, shop after shop. The sea breeze seemed to be tainted too; it carried the smell of the whole city, and the trees languished in the warm sun. It would have been lovely in the country this morning, but here it was almost unbearable. No wonder there is violence in these overcrowded cities, people living without trees and open fields. But even in the country there is violence. Man, wherever he lives, has become an enemy to himself and everything around him.

Let us leave the country and the cities and consider how each one of us is crowded with memories, hurts and the knowledge of a thousand years. We are, it appears, everlastingly occupied with something or other, inwardly or externally. Some with god, prayers and other theories; others with the affairs of the kitchen, the business of making money, with sex and with the welfare of animals; still others with politics and meditation, with research and the quiet life, with penury, and with the acquisition of things and knowledge. Why is it that we are almost never quiet with ourselves, to observe ourselves without any accustomed reactions? Why is it we don't watch our thoughts, the experiences, pleasant and unpleasant, that we have stored up? Why is it we follow the easiest and comforting course of life? Why is it we are so concerned about ourselves? Why is it that we are so appallingly selfish? This egotistic occupation is destroying us.